LONG DISTANCE RELATIONSHIPS

Learn How to Keep the Fire Improve Your Relationship

(The Ultimate Guide to Embracing and Strengthening Your Long Distance Relationship)

Michael Garcia

Published By **Michael Garcia**

Michael Garcia

All Rights Reserved

Long Distance Relationships: Learn How to Keep the Fire Improve Your Relationship (The Ultimate Guide to Embracing and Strengthening Your Long Distance Relationship)

ISBN 978-1-77485-420-4

All rights reserved. No part of this guide may be reproduced in any form without permission in writing from the publisher except in the case of brief quotations embodied in critical articles or reviews.

Legal & Disclaimer

The information contained in this book is not designed to replace or take the place of any form of medicine or professional medical advice. The information in this book has been provided for educational and entertainment purposes only.

The information contained in this book has been compiled from sources deemed reliable, and it is accurate to the best of the Author's knowledge; however, the Author cannot guarantee its accuracy and validity and cannot be held liable for any errors or omissions. Changes are periodically made to this book. You must consult your doctor or get professional medical advice before using any of the suggested remedies, techniques, or information in this book.

Upon using the information contained in this book, you agree to hold harmless the Author from and against any damages, costs, and expenses, including any legal fees potentially resulting from the application of any of the information provided by this guide. This disclaimer applies to any damages or injury caused by the use and application, whether directly or indirectly, of any advice or information presented, whether for breach of contract, tort, negligence, personal injury, criminal intent, or under any other cause of action.

You agree to accept all risks of using the information presented inside this book. You need to consult a professional medical practitioner in order to ensure you are both able and healthy enough to participate in this program.

TABLE OF CONTENTS

INTRODUCTION 1

CHAPTER 1: BUILDING A FAVORABLE LONG-DISTANCE DATE 2

CHAPTER 2: "TRUST ME" 6

CHAPTER 3: DECIDE ON WAYS TO REMAIN IN CONTACT . 12

CHAPTER 4: REASSURANCE 15

CHAPTER 5: ENJOY FUN THINGS TOGETHER AND APART . 21

CHAPTER 6: THE LONG-DISTANCE RELATIONSHIP THE CHALLENGE 37

CHAPTER 7: TECHNIQUES FOR MAKING THE LONG DISTANCE RELATIONSHIPS WORK 51

CHAPTER 8: WHAT TO DESIGN YOUR LONG-DISTANCE-DISTANCE-DATING WORK 62

CHAPTER 9: HOW TO MAKE YOUR LDRS WORK 66

CHAPTER 10: TIPS FOR SUSTAIN LONG-DISTANCE RELATIONSHIP 69

CHAPTER 11: REALISM ABOUT THE NEXT STEP 87

CHAPTER 12: PROBLEMS 93

CHAPTER 13: PLAN, TALK AND TALK ABOUT SHARE 98

CHAPTER 14: RECONNECTING WITH AN EXTENSIVE DISTANCE LOVER 103

CHAPTER 15: TIPS AND TRICKS FOR MAKING YOUR LOVE ONE LOVE YOU AND WANT TO BE WITH YOU EVEN WHILE HE/SHE IS ABSENT. 108

CHAPTER 16: SKYPE AND FACETIME 114

CHAPTER 17: ALWAYS MAINTAIN THE RIGHT ATTITUDE, THINK POSITIVE, DON'T BE JEALOUS AND YOU'LL BE CONTENT.. 119

CHAPTER 18: THE VISITS... 121

CHAPTER 19: STAY IN CONTACT EVERY DAY 129

CHAPTER 20: FINDING BALANCE.................................... 144

CHAPTER 21: THE LONG-DISTANCE RELATIONSHIP RECOMMENDATIONS.. 147

CHAPTER 22: THE DO'S AND DON'TS 164

CHAPTER 23: UTILIZE TECHNOLOGY TO CREATE AN "SHARED" EXPERIENCE... 169

CHAPTER 24: ALWAYS BE THERE FOR YOUR PARTNER .. 180

CONCLUSION.. 183

Introduction

This book provides the most effective steps and strategies on ways to help make your long-distance relationship successful. If you're considering entering into one, or you're already with one the book will offer you with helpful advice and insights on how to make it work.

It's true that being involved in long-distance relationships is not for the faint-hearted. It takes time, effort and a strong determination to get it done.

The good news is that you aren't required to go through it on your own. This book can you navigate the various aspects of your long-distance relationship. From creating trust, to improving communication, and discovering innovative ways to keep your romance going This book has got you covered.

Thank you so much for purchasing this book. I hope that you will enjoy it!

Chapter 1: Building A Favorable Long-Distance Date

There are ways to do it even from a distance to assure your spouse that you're on the same page for the long duration.

Keep your personal Skype or phone call schedules. The possibility of cancelling your spouse's Skype or phone calls could make them think that they're an option that isn't really an option in the event that nothing could be done. Make sure you keep your scheduled calls to Skype or phone whenever you want to go out on an opportunity to meet. After all, you're dating your spouse, right? Be sure to notify your family members or friends of your plans to spend the night with your spouse and to let them know that you're not available in the moment. If you have to cancel your plans due to emergencies, inform your spouse know that so they are not disturbed.

Discuss anything and everything. Be open about what you're feeling, talk about the things you are passionate about and the activities you're currently engaged in. Chat with your spouse using video chat, instant messenger, or email addresses. Send an old-fashioned note to your lover to surprise them or as an act of love. Send your spouse a small gift in the mailer you believe they'd like. It's the small things that will let them know you're thinking about them throughout your time off.

Visit each other regularly and don't cancel them until it's an emergency. In refusing to make a commitment to a planned visit or rescheduling your partner to go on a vacation could cause irreparable damage. By committing to your scheduled visits and commitments, you can show the other spouse that you are willing to see them often in the near future. If you aren't sure that your relationship is working or you have concerns about going to the restaurant in the future, talk about it with your spouse, rather than refusing to attend and denying the reason. The resolution of these issues will allow you to reconsider and build the relationship you have with your spouse.

Divide the costs of trips and discuss financial matters with your spouse. If your home is located at different points of the nation or Earth the financial situation must be discussed with regards to trips and planning to the next time. Are you a fiancee in a place where they don't make as much as you might? What is the fiance trying to cover in relation to trips? What do you want to see from the relationship with regard to financial matters in the future? Discussion of the financial aspects of your relationship can establish the foundation for the future, and help you establish agreements and commitments you want from your spouse.

Discuss where you are heading and the common goals. This allows each spouse to understand what it is they need be doing to make your relationship successful. This is particularly crucial when it comes to intercultural long-distance relationships. What are you looking for to achieve? What are your expectations? The obvious conclusion would be that at some point you'll be living together and eventually get married. Who is willing to relocate? Are you ready to move to a location that you can both agree on? Finding a common ground among the different cultures is essential for a successful intercultural relationship since it will avoid a lot of disputes in the future.

The relationship is a combination of spiritual, psychological physical, and financial investments. In general, long distance relationships may have a greater cost in these areas as compared to someone you meet regularly. Be honest to your spouse and make them aware of how much you truly care about them and inform them that something is bothering you. If your spouse is responsive with love and respect, you'll be able to build positive attributes for long-distance love and eventually close-distance romance.

Chapter 2: "Trust Me"

Trust is a crucial element in any relationship. No matter if your partner lives just within a single street and across oceans, without trust , a relationship won't last. So , how do you learn to trust your partner when you don't physically meet him daily?

If you were to meet your partner, trust needed to be earned . Now that you're in a long-distance relationship you must learn to let go of doubts and recall the trust you were able to build before you had an ongoing relationship. It takes time to establish trust in any relationship and can be achieved regardless of distance.

There isn't a simple method to build trust. It is a process that happens with time, however there are a variety of actions you can take to can help alleviate the fears and anxieties that can be a part of the long distance relationship.

No Secrets

It is crucial to not hide secrets from one another. There's a distinction between what you reveal and what you do not divulge. If you've been in a relationship for a long time and suddenly find themselves in a long distance relationship, you likely have a good idea of each other's secrets and won't have any issues discussing their past.

But, if you've only just started dating, like in the case of meeting on the internet, and you are just beginning your relationship it is crucial that you be honest and honest with one another. There is no need to share with your partner the entire story of your life or divulge your secrets in a flash However, at some point during your relationship, anything that could create friction should be discussed.

The actions speak louder than the words

Always do exactly what you've said you're going to do. For instance, if you have plans to be at in your home at a certain time for a video chat , and there is a problem that could result in you being late, contact us in advance and let them know why you'll not be available.

Be aware that it's usually the little gestures that to build trust in a relationship however, it's the little things that can rapidly destroy trust. If you keep your word, or calling before the deadline it is showing you and your spouse that you're trustworthy to keep your word.

Don't dwell on the past.

If you've been hurt in the past through your partner of choice or anyone else, by clinging to your anger and feelings of hurt, you'll gradually develop an uneasy relationship between you. It is essential not to think about the past. don't ram your past experiences in your partner's face. Do not dwell on events that have already occurred.

Focus your attention on the present moment and don't let your thoughts be distracted by things that might occur. Instead, concentrate on the good that can be made of your relationship. If you are focused on the negative, you could ultimately undermine the trust you have in your relationship. Focus on what's happening right now, not worrying about what could happen in the future.

Be honest

Whatever the hurt is, you must always keep the truth in mind. The fastest way to ruin any relationship is through lies. While telling the truth can be sometimes difficult, and certainly not always the first choice but it is the most secure way to ensure confidence.

If your partner is confident that you'll always be honest, whatever the consequence, they'll be more inclined to believe in them. If they hear your lying to others even if the lie isn't that big this is a sign to them that your can't be trusted.

Being honest can have negative consequences, but if your spouse realizes that you'll remain honest, regardless of the consequences there is a possibility that they will be angry at what you're truthful about, but they'll be confident in your integrity.

Communicate

One of the key aspects of building trust is to communicate with one another. Through being honest, asking questions, responding to questions, and discussing concerns about trust, you will build trust between you. It is crucial that you communicate with your partner regularly and share thoughts and feelings, and pay attention to each other's concerns.

You must talk to your partner like they were in the same room as you. Talk with them frequently and talk about even the smallest details of your day.

Be Realist

It is normal for long-distance relationships to be a source of conflict. Both parties must agree that you are separate. If one of you has to be concerned about what they're doing and with whom they are in every moment of the day this will place tension in your relationship, and ultimately destroy any trust you may have with one another.

If you're determined in making the relationship successful the two of you must be prepared to deal with the distance that separates you. If you both run at the first hint of trouble, your spouse will lose faith in you.

Have faith in yourself and your partner. If you're not apprehensive about your partner at every moment they are with you, why would you do it when they're an extended distance? Long distance relationships could alter your thinking but you shouldn't let negative thoughts affect the relationship. That's why you should trust your partner regardless of difference in distance.

Trust yourself to do only do the right decision. Before you can gain trust, you must be able to trust yourself. Make wise choices and stay clear of any tempting situations. If you are confident in your dreams and goals for the future together, you'll learn to build trust, and eventually increase your chances of an effective long-distance relationship.

Chapter 3: Decide On Ways To Remain In Contact

How often will you connect?

The scheduling of time to reconnect while you're not together is an additional element crucial for an effective LDR. In reality, it's the vitality of your relationship when you're living apart. Some couples prefer to communicate frequently every day. If you're not one those couples, ensure that you connect at least every couple of days and in a meaningful way.

What's the significance? This is dependent on each individual and is something that you must find out regarding your spouse. Certain people go for several days without having contact, and still feel very close to their loved ones. Some people require contact multiple times throughout the day to feel closer. You together with your partner must establish what you need in advance and make an agreement regarding how you'll foster feelings of intimacy.

What Methods Do You Choose to Use?

In this day and age of modern technology, it'd be a lie if anyone ever claims that the biggest obstacle to an LDR is communication techniques. A LDR couple should always be contact through various methods of communication. The wide array of online media options today, including text, cell phone and video chat, clearly makes it easier to maintain the connection and maintain closeness.

Luckily, technology has given people with LDRs various ways of contacting. What is the most effective one? This depends on the ones that will make you feel the most connected to your spouse. So, it is important to be aware of the kinds of interaction that you and your partner need as different people will prefer different forms of contact.

How often do you want to stay in touch using the way you prefer? Do you want to be in contact twice per day? Every day?

Twice per week? Every month? Now, take a few minutes to look over every communication method and choose the one you'll utilize as your means of keeping in touch.

Loving Questions to LDR Couples

You can rate each communication method on a scale from 1 to 5 one, with 1 being the most appealing and 5 being the most attractive. Decide the frequency you'd like to be in contact using this method.

1. What do you think of Texting?

2. How often do want to text?

3. How would you rate phone calls?

4. How often do want to speak on the phone?

5. What do you think of Video Chatting (Skype, Google Hangout, Facetime)?

6. How often do you need to video Chat?

7. What do you think of connecting via the social networks (Facebook, Twitter, etc.)?

8. How often do your want to make contact via social media?

Chapter 4: Reassurance

Things we consider to be normal in our everyday lives could get overlooked when you're two people living different lives. For instance, you might miss a call, or might not be able call your loved ones when you're in the middle of a class or when something other is going on. It is a good idea to establish a policy among you, that blank message is a sign that you're not able to answer calls at this time however, you're fine. It is also possible to make use of smileys to show that you're sorry that you aren't able to talk in the present however life gets busy. You can use symbols that you are familiar with to indicate that you are:

I am working, but will contact you once I'm done.

I am working for the boss.

It is a class

I'm driving the car.

These are small messages of assurance which you can deliver even when things are hectic. If you are unable to, then take every opportunity to send these messages so that your loved person isn't left in the dark, wondering whether you've lost touch with them. The feeling of loneliness is extremely difficult to bear when your loved person is from home. If you are certain that you've committed an error, don't wait to start calling, but ensure that you make it clear immediately and prove your credibility so that your loved ones can trust your commitment to them. That's vital.

It is possible that your loved ones could be thinking:

* Is the child okay?

* Have they been involved in an accident?

Has she/he come across another person?

Like you had an obligation to keep your parents up-to-date on your movements when you were a young child and you must think about the thoughts that might be running through your loved one's head even if you've never replied to an email or text and, even if this requires setting up responses to ensure that there's no doubt as to what you're doing. The decision to turn off the phone could cause your loved one to be very scared as they feel alone in a moment when more reassurance is needed. This extra effort can go a long ways in aiding your loved one to remove doubts. Remember that your absence is already bad enough, and you don't need to compound it with a insufficient response time.

Emotional reactions

If you're in a relationship, where you interact with your partner every day and you are in a relationship that is not a constant one, you may not require the same amount of emotional support. It could be beneficial to leave something behind for your loved ones that they will feel reassured by even when you're not there. Maybe record a text message. Maybe even gift them something precious to you, to reassure them that you're always in the process to return. In this instance it is important to understand that they do not have them in their lives, and the loneliness of being in a lonely space can be brutal. So, go excessive with your words of encouragement. It's not a bad idea to give flowers or an e-card to let them know you love them even if you talk frequently. Every little gesture helps your loved one feel secure and can help connect you.

Michael and Alice were forced to split due to his job circumstances. The situation for Alice was not any better, and she was in her home all day, waiting for Michael to call or provide some indication that he'd return. Michael came up with an idea for her to make sure she would have something to keep her busy. He's always wanted to have to knit a sweater at home and while she knit it, she felt energized and connected to Michael. If you can imagine something similar to that is a great idea, as it helps alleviate the loneliness that comes with having a partner who is who is a long distance away.

Making plans together is good because Skype calls and phone calls aren't just regular calls. These are the dates you will have with your beloved and it is important to plan them and make them special instead of being just a chat between acquaintances. If she is able to see that you've got her photo on your phone or demonstrate to him an email he wrote to her via Skype it will help to keep the love the two of you feel for one another. It's not just about breaking news. It's more about comfort and connection. Skype calls can help to feel as if you're close, even if miles have separated you.

Avoid doing anything that could be considered an unintentionally jealous manner. The issue in this situation is it demonstrates the lack of confidence. For instance, in Ian and Katy's case, Katy showed on every Skype phone call the fact that she was jealous girls on campus along with her boyfriend. At the end of the day the man was so annoyed by his accusations, they fell away. In any relationship that's going be lasting, there needs the need for trust. Remember that it's the absence of each other that suggests that you're living different lives. You shouldn't take one another's fault for having a good time in the life. This isn't fair and absurd. It's okay to have fun. Have fun and share your joy. Put jealousy aside because it's not appropriate in a relationship that is long distance. If jealousy comes out be assured that the relationship won't last.

Chapter 5: Enjoy Fun Things Together And Apart

Once you've determined the method by which you'll contact one another and how frequently you'll have to figure out what you'll be doing while communicating. To keep your long distance relationship going, a simple video chats could become boring sometimes. It is therefore essential to discover additional things that you can talk about with your partner in order to spice your love life.

In LDRs the fun isn't just an option, it's extremely satisfying and gives you the feeling of belonging. However is the fact that it's another element of the foundation of an LDR relationship. Being happy and smiling while having fun while also discovering common interests - all of these are possible in LDRs to ensure both of you can continue to enjoy each other and grow as an individual. There are many ways to have a great time even when you're not in the same room.

High-quality Conversation Topics

Every day, you talk to your partner and become acquainted but what happens when you're running out of ideas to discuss? A good topic will help you grow in your exploration of your companion. Here are a few questions you could ask your partner every day that will encourage you to engage in conversations, sharing and sharing more fully. An effective method to keep conversations flowing can be to pose the question and then listen to the answer, follow up with "why?" to find out more.

Questions about your Favorite Sites

What's your favourite holiday? Why?

What is your most loved type of TV show, movie, or book?

What is your most-loved food type (Chinese, Mexican, Mediterranean)?

What is your most-loved meal of this kind of food?

What is your preferred method to enjoy yourself in a large city?

What is your most favorite method to enjoy the natural world?

What is your most favorite sport? To be a part of?

What's your top app?

What is your most favorite web site?

Who is your favorite comedian/singer/athlete/musician/politician?

Which is your most loved family member?

Who is your coworker with whom you work the most?

What is your top cook?

Questions regarding Past Experiences

Where did you grow up?

Where were you raised?

How was your family when you were a young child?

Which was your most loved family member as a child?

What was it like being when you were a teen?

What were the most memorable and worst aspects of high school?

Did you attend college? If yes how was it?

What was your most memorable accomplishment as a young adult, teenager or child?

What are your most regrettable moments as a teenager, young adult or child?

What is your best memory from your childhood or youth?

Do you have any events that occurred in your life that you should be aware of?

Concerns about Future Dreams

What do you wish to be in the near future?

What are your career and job goals?

Do you have plans to tie the knot in the near future?

Do you have a desire to start an unison in the future?

What do you think of the ownership of a home?

Where do you plan to travel to in the near future?

If you had the chance to travel around the world Where should you travel to? Why?

What are your hopes and dreams regarding your finances?

What are your goals for your family?

What do you think of your what life will be like in retirement?

Questions just for fun

Do you enjoy surprises? Do you remember the time you were shocked and what transpired?

If you had an extraordinary power What would you choose to use it for? Why?

Who do you consider your hero? Why?

If you had the chance to be a professional athlete which one would you choose? Why?

If you were to have 10 million dollars what could you possibly do?

If you could own any vehicle, what would you choose?

If you could own a house how would it be like?

Choices to Fun Together Online

This section you will find many activities you can do with your partner while they "hang out" on the internet. Take a look and get the most enjoyment from your time together by engaging in things that are fun!

Take a turn playing a video game. A lot of couples play video games together and it's certainly an enjoyable activity. There are numerous game-based websites that offer multiplayer games on the internet. Some are completely free, and others require a fee. Some of the best online game services are available at: https://games.yahoo.com, http://www.zapak.com, http://www.agame.com, and a lot more. Make sure to play multiplayer games on Facebook.

Watch a show: With Netflix or other sites to watch an episode of a show or film with your family. Being able to laugh with your partner at the hilarious scenes and gasp over the gruesome shots will make the distance go by. Relax on the couch in a comfortable chair and relax for the evening by being with your loved one.

Read a book: Couples can have their own Book Club for Two. Reading together in two different places is a lot of enjoyable. This is ideal for people who love reading. The goal is to locate the book that you are interested in and then read it in your the time you have free, but separately. Then, you can talk about the book, one chapter at each chapter. This will lead to lots of discussion. Look up the title of the book online and you'll find its own website that has discussions questions and more. Learning is always beneficial within the context of an LDR relationship.

Sing Karaoke: Do you love music? Do you enjoy singing? For those who don't, this could seem odd initially however, it's quite a fun way to have an unique place to hang out. There are several websites that provide online karaoke, with the possibility of duet. For instance, http://www.singsnap.com is a free service that gives you the platform to sing together. The act of singing is beneficial for your soul, and it's also great for sharing moments of laughter. Karaoke is a fantastic method to feel happy and have a blast!

Listen to music: They claim, "Music is to the soul what words do to the brain." If you're couples living far away an effective method to bond would be to listen to some great music! There are many websites that offer online streaming services, such as, http://www.live365.com, http://www.grooveshark.com and they are a good place to find your favorite songs online. You and your partner can make the radio stations of your choice using services such as http://blip.fm. Finding your favorite artists music, genres, and tracks is a great method to connect and enjoy yourself while having fun.

Plan an Outing If you're in an LDR likely enjoy traveling. If that's the case then why not make an upcoming trip to meet one another? Perhaps even better, you can plan your own trips you'd like to go on when you're married in the near future. Through the virtual tour, you'll be able to go to any place on the internet. Check out .http://www.360cities.net because it is a website where you can find a location that you long to visit and go through a virtual tour together!

Cooking together Do you enjoy cooking together? consume food? If you're located in different regions of the world, take pleasure in the culinary delights. Cooking can be fun and is considered to be an art. It takes an exotic meal amount of time to cook and a couple might decide to spend a night cooking together while video chatting. All you need to do is connect the webcam and cook your own food. The recipe should be shared in advance so your guests can follow the recipe. It's a chance to try something new, try an entirely new recipe, and then share an evening with someone you cherish.

Create Your Love Story: LDRs are among the most romantic stories there! You give up your love for one another and keep the love affair going even when things are difficult. If you can spend a weekend together with one your partner, it can turn into an unforgettable romance. Record it in your diary! Using https://drive.google.com/ you and your partner can both write and add to your love story as it happens. The highs! The lows! The landmarks and the darkness.

Make Some Art: Are you either of you artistic? Do you enjoy visual media? If so, you'll be able to create a masterpiece on your own. Select a theme, pick an online platform and start with! Look into Fresh Paint, an app for Windows or other apps similar to it. It is possible to make it with friends or you can each create one and then compare. It's a fun activity to do while video-chatting.

Start a Savings Account The idea is for couples who intend to stay together in the long run. This is a great way to begin to save money that you can spend for your love life, whether that's cash for trips or to be used when you begin to live together in the future term. Placing money in a bank account is also a sign of trust. You're attempting to test the waters of financial stability with a low risk. An effective method to start is to commit to putting into the same amount each month regardless of whether it's $25 per month. At the end of the year, you'll have $600, money you'll need to fund any future activities you decide to undertake together.

You can have a baby: Although being a parent is the ultimate goal for the couple who is married A virtual baby can be an ideal test ground for couples who are in an extended relationship. If you live in different places, you are able to adopt the role of a virtual baby. This can be achieved through a website, such as, http://www.cyberinfants.com. Discussion topics that result from this enjoyable and interactive game can teach you something about yourself and your child's potential parents.

These methods are among the best ways to enjoy yourself and keep in touch with your spouse in an extended relationship. make conversations as enjoyable as they can be. The more that a couple spends time together, having fun, sharing knowledge, and broadening their knowledge and experiences, the more it can aid in defining a long and lasting relationship.

Sending a Special Gift to your Lover

Your partner and you won't be always in touch however, you can still perform a variety of things to demonstrate your feelings for one another and strengthen your relationship even when you're not together. Consider ways to make your partner feel special and happy. You might think that you must send something, invest an enormous amount of money, make a statement or the right thing to earn your lover's affection however that could not be any further from the truth!

Video Messages: Even if aren't in a particular area along with an LDR partner or friend, you can record short videos on your mobile phone while you're there. Video in which you add a few words of love or something you enjoy, and send it. It will show them that you'd love to have them and will give them a glimpse of your day.

Cards: In recent times cards have become an essential for couples who have been separated for a while. Our era is no different. Virtual or snail mail it is a great feeling for everyone when they receive a gift card with a thoughtful message from a loved ones. There are several free e-card website, such as, www.123greetings.com, www.bluemountain.com,

http://www.kisseo.com,

www.americangreetings.com, etc. These websites are able to be utilized for sending greeting cards to loved ones. It is important to regularly send your feelings through a card can help in keeping the romance alive.

Flowers Sending flowers is expensive, therefore it might not be feasible in the moment. The most effective option is to go with something that is virtual. One example is to send a virtual bouquet of flowers. There are websites that offer such services, like, http://www.virtualflowers.com (Virtual Flowers) through which one can send customized virtual flower bouquet free-of-cost. Another site that deserves mention is http://www.flowers2mail.com.

LDR Bracelet as a long-distance couple, you and your partner ought to be proud of the possibility to remain close even though you live in different places. An excellent way to express an euphoria can be to put on something like an LDR bracelet. It lets others know about the kind of relationship you're engaged in. It can also give an emotional boost to your spirits when you notice it in your wrist. LDR Bracelet can be purchased at various prices, and the purchase price is dependent on the individual and depends on the budget you have set. The site, https://www.etsy.com

is the most likely location to browse for an LDR bracelet. There are many designs available to pick from. This website also sells inexpensive bracelets: http://www.lovingfromadistance.com/ldrbracelets.html.

Handmade Gifts: Are You creative? Do you paint, draw or sew, weld or write? If you're a person with the ability to be creative and are a bit of a genius, you're in luck. The most meaningful presents are ones you design by yourself. The fact that you put in the effort to create it yourself can have a profound impact on the person you're with.

There are a variety of things LDR partners can give to each other, small different small gifts that will help to light romance. It doesn't matter if it's a video or a gift that is simple that shows your love can help keep the bonds that are strong.

LOVE QUESTIONS FOR LDR Couples

1. What are your thoughts when you ask an Question of the Day?

2. What time would you like to inquire and then discuss the matter?

3. Which of the online games are most appealing to you? What do you want to explore?

4. What online activity would you like to try first?

5. Which is the items on the list would you prefer to stay clear of?

6. Would you prefer to receive an item or a video or both from your spouse?

7. Are there items that aren't listed you'd like to get? If yes, what's it?

8. Which of the presents from the list would you rather not be gifted?

Chapter 6: The Long-Distance Relationship The Challenge

A relationship that is long-distance can be a challenge. Numerous reasons could lead to couples living in different locations for a variety of reasons, including working abroad or studying in different areas. But, it should not be a reason to avoid. Under normal circumstances relationship relationships can face a variety of challenges and it's up to the partners to work together as a group to overcome these challenges.

Sometimes , you make the "what you would do" list. It's true that the long-distance relationship can be challenging. Keep in mind that if the two of you had the ability to over come obstacles and hurdles to find the love and joy you are entitled to. In the end, distance tests your love for one another. Once you're finally united all the battles and hurdles you faced to keep the love in check will be over.

Here are a few of the problems that must be overcome:

1. You'd like them to respond quickly

It occurs to almost all couples. It is among the most common problems encountered in long-distance relationships. For instance, you may have sent a text or phone call to your loved ones, but they didn't respond.

In the near future, you could encounter a situation in which everything about your spouse is suspicious. You might be hesitant to believe the relationship for no reason at all.

There are times where you feel lonely in your relationship and you wonder why relationships that are long distance don't work.

Way Out.

It is important to recognize that these thoughts are not yours and reality may differ from what you think.

It's not necessarily a sign that it's a sign that something is wrong in the event that your partner doesn't respond. You must remain patient, and wait until they will become free and respond to your messages and phone calls.

Doubts about a long-distance relationship is common. But if doubts continue to recur the more likely that the issue lies with you and not with your partner.

Talking too long

This characteristic is prevalent for couples who just begun their long-distance romance. This is something couples who are new to love are looking for.

Why can't they communicate for hours? It's the sole way to keep their friendship alive!

It might look nice initially. But when the relationship becomes older and you both stick to the habit of chatting or talking throughout the day and at the night, this behavior is soon categorized among the most annoying issues that arise in relationships with distant partners.

Way Out

If you're hoping to have a long-lasting relationship, you should keep it in check. Of course, you have to keep in touch and discuss everything you know about yourself with your spouse.

However, it doesn't need long conversations. A well-balanced and thoughtful conversation in the duration of a few minutes will give enormous advantages in the long term.

A break for the remainder of your life

If you feel you and your partner are slipping away, it is one of the most crucial problems in a relationship that you should look out for!

Do you keep your mobile phone at hand? Do you feel like everything seems to have stopped? Do you feel as if there's nothing you can do even when you're not with each other?

If you do then, over time the issues that you create for yourself are likely to become more severe. If you become more involved in your relationship than needed, you'll become depressed.

Long-distance relationships can be difficult. The fact that you aren't taking care of your personal and social life can cause depression and anxiety.

That could cause problems in your relationships with people who live far away.

Way Out

Don't let your life be centered solely around your relationship. Instead, explore other interests take part in new activities, and, most importantly, develop your career!

This will enhance your overall quality of life and, consequently improve your happiness and more healthy relationship with your spouse.

Almost no deep communication

Relationship issues that are long distance can result in less intimate communications. The general perception is that there's not much to say, and that conversations are merely superficial.

Life-threatening and important problems must be discussed However, it is often difficult to know how the day went , and yet the deep communication goes absent.

This happens because the two of them don't have the same view of their lives. It is common for people to believe that their companions don't comprehend what they're going through, even though they are sharing the same experience.

People with long-distance relationships are more able to talk about their daily issues with colleagues or friends who have physical contact.

Way Out

Despite these ongoing issues Every couple should be conscious of how they be more in touch for a happier as well-balanced relationship.

Make a plan for a Zoom date and remember to dress the same way you would for a traditional date!

This is essential to reduce the distance. Therefore, think outside the box and utilize technology to stay connected and enjoy a pleasant conversation.

Insecurity

This is another one of the most frequent long-distance relationships issues.

It's normal for fears to surface. If it happens ask your friend to soothe you.

However, when it comes to relationships that span distances making contact with your spouse when your thoughts turn to him will not be easy.

Insecure relationships can cause jealousy and can undermine relationship that exists between your spouse and you.

Way Out

Significant uncertainties are ones that should be dealt with early enough to prevent any further problems. Finding solutions to problems in relationships with long distances should always be handled in groups.

If, for any reason, you or your spouse doesn't feel secure, don't let the issue go unnoticed and develop into a habit. Talk about it when you're both feeling relaxed.

Do not force your partner to do anything or trigger anger. It could cause irreparable damage which cannot be repaired. Be patient and accept the situationwith maturity, and act and resolve the issue.

Misunderstandings

There are always miscommunications in every relationship. The more serious issue is the actual issue.

Have you ever wondered how to deal with long-distance relationships problems after a disagreement after a long distance road gets hard and you've considered a variety of psychologists and personality theories but no solution was found.

What do I do?

If you're unsure You should rethink your decision. Accept your errors.

Talk to your partner and be able to understand the confusion before you contact the psychologist.

In no doubt, experts can assist with your issues, but keep in mind that at the end of the day, it's only you and your spouse. It is impossible to improve anything without your consent.

Not paying attention to other relationships important to you

Troubles with relationships that are long distance can be a sign of ignoring other people.

Do you like to spend your spare moment on the phone conversing with your partner?

If it is, this is a red signal. You are not focusing on other relationships and focused on your relationship with love.

Way Out

You'll need a group of friends. You must connect to your loved ones and always be there for them when they require you.

If you're looking to lead a fulfilled life, don't forget those that are significant to you. This could include your friends and siblings, or even others; they are your beneficiaries.

Stonewalling

Stonewalling is among the most common issues encountered in long-distance relationships. It can be a hassle for people who suffer from it!

Imagine how stressful it could be to not receive a phone call or text message from your partner for a long time without feeling guilt-ridden! It may not be the separation however, your partner's behavior could cause uncertainty, confusion and anger.

Way Out

Even if you are feeling very unhappy stones should not be considered a viable option.

If you simply sweep the issues away and offer your partner a peaceful snack, you'll get further than you are.

When you're in a relationship with someone intimate, it's simple to bridge physical distance. However, once you break up emotionally, it can be a challenge to get back into the relationship.

Additionally, it's important to address the disagreements early enough to avoid your relationship from going down an unforgiving path.

Gaslighting

Another problem that is often encountered when it comes to long-distance relationships is the gaslighting.

Many people love to play games with their family members and play games with debt and make their loved ones feel guilty because of something they've not done!

This is a way to emphasize their importance to their partner. A lot of people use gaslighting when they're uncertain and wish their partner to be always dependent on their ideas.

However, it's unhealthy. This isn't love!

The consequences of gaslighting that is not stopped could be severe and cause major issues. The victim may become exhausted and the relationship isn't altered.

It is possible to lose your passion for life due to minor issues with your ego and this unhealthy practice of gazing.

Way Out

If you switch the on to someone else, you should stop turning it off immediately when you see it. If needed, get assistance from a professional.

If your spouse is guilty, you can explain your consequences. Reassure them that they do not have to control you in order to save your life.

You may also consider seeking couples therapy to solve your problems and rebuild your relationship.

Cheating

One of the most common issues in relationships that are long distance is cheating. Because people have needs and secondly, it's simple to conceal your partner from you.

It is sometimes difficult to open up in their relationships at a distance and share their emotions and concerns.

The moment when people begin to feel a connection with someone physically available and readily accessible. While not realizing it, they transcend limits of friendship, and start to feel romantic.

It's called emotional infidelity. However, sometimes, people simply need a physical connection.

There is no need to fall in love to do this. This could result in romantic relationships, single-night dates or even friendships that have advantages!

Way Out

No matter the motive the reason, cheating isn't acceptable in relationships. To avoid infidelity within your relationship, you must do all you can to stay contact with your spouse.

You can play with various privacy-related apps, play sex games and get together frequently as you can.

Individuals who have long-distance relationships face challenges.

However, if you truly love someone and you practice open and truthful communication, distance won't really matter.

When you've identified a serious issue, it's important to solve it before it becomes bothering you.

If you're unable to resolve the issue yourself, but you would like to repair them, consider hiring a professional to fix them.

A licensed counselor or therapist is the ideal person to assess your situation, find the root problems, and offer an honest assessment on your relationships.

Chapter 7: Techniques For Making The Long Distance Relationships Work

If you're familiar of the many pitfalls faced by partners in a long distance relationships and have looked into the issues that may be emerging within your own LDR It's time to address the issues and improve the relationship. Making a long-distance relationship work isn't a particularly scientific process. It's all about doing small, meaningful things that keep your loved one content and hopeful. It's not uncommon for those who live far apart to be lonely and long for attention. Therefore, it is important to be there for them when they require you and let them know them that you're satisfied to be with them. In depth, the tips and steps below will help you to streamline and improve your long-distance relationships.

Feel special for your partner Every day, try to discover something, no matter how tiny, you could accomplish to make your partner feel like you are thinking of them.

It could be as simple as saying , 'I enjoy talking to you' or 'You make my day'. Whatever the case that you say, these small gestures will make people feel good, especially than in long-distance relationships that don't have the opportunity to visit you as frequently as they'd prefer.

Some of the partners in highly successful long distance relationships have spoken about email photos of themselves, handwritten letters , and small gifts. The key is to be imaginative. It's not necessary to use the same channels of communication to stay connected with your loved ones to let them know you appreciate them. Give them a surprise in the present and future. Send an antique item to remind them of how much you love and cherish their love and appreciation. It is also helpful when you're interested in the interests of your partner. If you came across an online article you think they'd enjoy, you can give your partner a copy. It will serve to remind them that, even as you are going about your daily routine you're still thinking of them. So, they'll be benefited, and your relationship will grow tremendously positively. Simple things can mean a lot.

Trust one another - trust is among those essential elements that are required in any relationship that is described as healthy. However, lots of people who are in long-distance relationships are prone to issues with trust. In general, as a rule of rule of thumb, don't trust your partner in the event that they've provided you with a reason to! Are they unfaithful at times? If they haven't, then don't doubt them. Nothing is more sinister than accusing someone of committing fraud even though they're innocent. If you're going to bring any allegations, you must be certain. Many people come to the mistake of thinking that their partner has been cheating because they're not doing what they want from them. It's not true.

What should you do should you do if you suspect your spouse is being unfaithful to you, and would like to know more? Many people take the snoopy approach in the quest to find the cheating spouse. However, that isn't the way to do it. So, there's no need to be hacking into their email or obtaining the details of their texts without their permission. It would be intruding on their privacy and be considered to be disrespectful. If you're engaged it is important to discuss everything with your spouse. This means that everything is open to discussion. How can you simply inquire if they are cheating, without being accusatory? So, let me ask like "If you've ever been caught cheating on mebefore, could you be willing to let me know If your spouse responds 'yes' and you're sure to be fine. However, if they offer an answer like "why would you want to know to do that?', then they're probably being defensive. This could suggest they're trying to cover something up however don't be too quick to accuse them at this point. Just tell them that you're interested, and if they persist in being defensive and attempting to avoid this line of conversation You might move to ask them if they've ever been cheated.

Prepare for the future being anxious about the future is a common problem for couples who are who live far apart. It's also important to recognize that long distance relationships aren't casual. Of course, you're being in a relationship due to the fact that you love the person. It shouldn't be a problem for them to move to your place or in reverse. But, you can move to accommodate one another. If you are truly in love with the person you are with, moving to a new address should not be that difficult. LDRs are not the same as cities in which a relationship could begin as casual and eventually turn into something more serious. Long distance relationships need to be a serious relationship, which means both of you have plans for the future. This can help eliminate any of the doubts and worries that either of you has.

Visit often - frequent visits are a wonderful feature in a long distance relationship.

Make a plan for dates. It will give both of you something to anticipate. It's likely to cost a lot for you both to travel to your partner's home So you must be prepared for the cost. You may want to cut back on some money. Whatever the reason it is important to keep in mind is that it's important to travel to show love, and to visit your loved ones frequently as often as is feasible. In general however, ensure that you can afford the trip before spending your entire savings.

Communicate regularly . Some couples who are in long-distance relationships can communicate for as long as once a day. This may not be enough for you. It could be very extreme. However, talking to them once every couple of weeks can be also extreme! If you're able to make an effort to stay on the phone every day and figure out the length of time that is appropriate for you to spend in contact with them. There are some people who have more busy schedules than the others and there isn't a'magic time frame' for you to be at the end of the line. Find something that is beneficial for you both in terms of communicating and staying contact. If you're struggling with paying phone bills, it is possible to search for companies that have lower rates even if that means the two of you switching. There are businesses that give free calls within their network.

Make sure you have an internet service and a webcam. This could be a bit too expensive for you if you're in your teens and your parents don't want to pay for high-speed internet. However, if you're able get it, it will help a good amount to have an internet connection that is reliable, as well as a quality webcam. If you can purchase these things you should consider it. It is essential to have the most enjoyable time when you're communicating with your friend via video-calling platforms like Skype. While your smartphone may allow you to make video calls occasionally keep be in mind that a webcam can facilitate more interaction. It allows you to study your loved one's body language and watch how they express themselves. Interactions can be an enjoyable method to connect. They can also be a great way to get a head start for those who don't have much to say. Additionally, you'll be able to learn a lot about your partner's and their body language.

Don't be afraid to voice your concerns There's nothing wrong with being anxious about certain aspects of long-distance relationships. If you are facing uncertainties about infidelity, or your future together, who better to address them than your boyfriend/girlfriend?

You have also a life - for certain people, it's easy to become completely absorbed in your love life, to the point that you forget about your family and friends. Even though you'll likely spend much of your time in your relationship, you should not forget about your connections to others. It's fine to decline acquaintances every now and then when you're planning a date with your partner, however, it's not something you need to repeat it every time. However try not to make your partner feel like they're less important than your peers.

The benefits of date nights are that you make sure you have them whenever you can. It is best to schedule an evening of date nights every week. Even if you live from each other doesn't mean that you shouldn't be able to meet up. Try watching the same film simultaneously or even eat the same food.

How to handle arguments - naturally it happens in every healthy relationship. The key difference is the way you handle conflict and arguments in a relationship that is long distance. To make sure you're following the correct procedure Here are some principles to keep in mind:

Don't put down the phone when you are fighting, you might be tempted to shut off the phone. However, don't do it. This is disrespectful and nobody is entitled to it. Try to keep to it. Consider making a commitment to one another that neither of you will ever leave the phone.

Don't interrupt and do not interrupt your partner while they're talking about some thing. Make sure you listen to each other's explanations.

It's crucial to listen to what the person is actually sayingeven if you think you're not. Do not dismiss their ideas simply because you don't pay attention. demonstrate respect.

• Say your feelings and not the things they did. Rather instead of blaming them just say the actions they took made you feel.

* Find a compromise in the event that both parties agree to disagree There is always a way to compromise. You can agree on something you're confident about. It could mean that you don't necessarily get exactly what you want.

Don't give your partner the cold shoulder. This is a bad idea that is probably more damaging than just hanging up. If it doesn't be a good thing it's better not to do it.

* Don't delay any conflict. If there's a dispute that requires taking care of,

resolve it as quickly as you can. It's much better to resolve it and get it over with. Remember that the longer you put off the issue the more impact it has on the two of you.

* Don't get too excited about distance. It's normal for people who are in relationships with long distances to be upset and then start an argument. The first thing to do is stop arguing and you'll save yourself many headaches.

Do not argue on the internet If you're in a disagreement, it's better to have a discussion instead of arguing on Skype or on Facebook.

Chapter 8: What To Design Your Long-Distance-Distance-Dating Work

It's difficult to maintain loyalty when two people are separated, and maintaining relationships becomes more difficult the longer the relationship persists. Insecurities usually occur because one person may not be sure of what the other person is doing, etc. However, the truth of the matter is that long-distance relationships are able to function just as other relationships. However, relationship isn't easy and requires commitment from both people involved. Here you will find some ideas on how to strengthen your bond with your partner.

Beware of Communicating Too Much

The standards regarding what is considered to be excessively frequent communication varies from couple to. There are two extremes one of which is the couple that communicates too often and the couple who do not communicate in sufficient amounts. It is not necessary to cover the distance by binding one another with jealousy. Some couples are able to remain silent for three times, and stay together for over 30 years and there are couples who communicate every hour, and then break up after two weeks. The most effective approach is to follow the flow and follow what's normal for the relationship.

Beware of Serious or Bad Situations

To avoid bad situations, you should be aware of things that could cause a problem for your spouse. Since they are absent, it's more stressful for a relationship when you go out with someone from the past or have a drink with friends, but you are fully aware of the fact that it might upset your spouse.

There are two choices to consider in risky scenarios: either you avoid moving at all , or you notify your friend or partner about your plans prior to departure, giving them enough time to assure them or her.

Be sure to keep your girlfriend, boyfriend or spouse. in your mind prior to making certain decisions.

Do Things Together

This could mean various things. In our Technologically-dependent society, you might choose to consider playing online video games or watching YouTube videos together. You can also read exactly the same texts, Skype, movies, and more. in the distance. Even though you're separated from one another, that does not mean you shouldn't talk about bonds and experiences.

Meet the Other

Your relationship must be a two-way street. Naturally, you won't be able to move without having a relationship throughout your lives. Therefore, visits are essential. Additionally, you will have more enjoyable time when you see one another again. If you're the sole one who has a go to make a difference, then the person likely become resentful of each other.

Be Fair

Furthermore, it is simple to deny or alter the truth from your loved one when you have a lot in common because they're not trying to convince you of something they are not. But, no relationship can be built with lies, which means the best option you can make for your relationship is to be honest to one another.

Chapter 9: How To Make Your Ldrs Work

Relationships with long distances are more prevalent when individuals travel for study, work or due to reasons that are beyond their control. Although it's never easy but it is possible to ensure that relationships flourish regardless of distance. Here are some of my recommendations to build relationships that last ...

Plan your long-distance relationship

Make time for a the courage to have a serious, honest conversation together with the person you love. Consider any challenges that you may have to confront while you're from each other. Talk openly about what is going on . Plan how you will respond when things happen, as is likely to happen. Create contingency plans to deal with your sexual fears, insecurities and what you'll have to do to help your relationship flourish. The people who are successful in long-distance relationships don't leave anything to chance. The process of planning strengthens your commitment to the relationship and determination to succeed.

Make sure that the communication channels remain open

When you're hundreds or even thousands of miles away it's not difficult to be a bit "separate". Effective relationships over long distances require daily interactions and exchanges ("against one another"). It is a the obligation to speak to each other on a regular basis. Set a daily time to connect with each other. Whatever the duration, even if it's only 30 minutes a day, it's important to keep the relationship alive. Be sure that the time you select is completely yours and there isn't any kind of distraction.

Make use of all essential communication tools. Texts, phones, emails and postal mail cameras ... it is your responsibility to must to utilize all of them. Keep in mind that there's an order of value in these communication tools. It is recommended to make use of an array of communication tools to ensure that you are able to communicate with one another. Emails and texts are great for notes that are short however, they are more effective because they are very susceptible to being misinterpreted. Send gifts, pictures or music videos made by hand and love letters from the past. There's nothing like receiving a gift from a loved one who is far away and it lets your loved one know how much you love them and think of them.

Say your heartfelt words of love to your partner. Let them know that you cherish you even though it would seem obvious. Say the words to them and say it repeatedly.

Chapter 10: Tips For Sustain Long-Distance Relationship

In order to make it through the short-term or long-term - long separation, you have to remain focused and determined. Here, then, are few suggestions for making it.

#1: Make plans with your partner

The first and most effective option you can make for long distance relationships is to organize things in advance. How will you maintain contact? via email, phone... and Facebook? What frequency will you communicate with one another? Are you willing to chat at specific times of the week, or only whenever your schedule allows it? Are there plans where you could meet face to face or could it be impossible? These are important questions to be asked, as it isn't a good idea to have one expecting regular contact while the other is hoping for an instant chat every week. Therefore, you should plan your schedule so that you can determine what your positions are in these important questions.

Set aside time for an honest and intimate conversation together with your companion. Accept all difficulties you're likely to encounter because of being so different from each your partner. Talk about all the "what ifs" and determine what you'll do if they happen, as they will. Create contingency plans to deal with your anxieties, sexual desires, and the steps you must implement to ensure the relationship continues to flourish. The couples who are successful in their relationships over long distances do not abandon things to chance. If you plan ahead, you can strengthen your commitment to each other and increase the confidence to keep it going.

If you're in a relationship that lasts for a long time there is a great likelihood that you'd like to stay with the person for the remainder all your days. So, you need to start having conversations with them about the future. This is a great method to make sure that both of you are looking forward to something when the distance has been decreased to zero.

The concepts don't require seriousness in the beginning. It's great to have something you can discuss and work to achieve. Talk about where you're going to be living, how your home is going to appear like, and what you plan to do together. Talk about things like what you'll cook your dinner together or what you'll buy when you go out shopping together. There are no limits to what you can do. The possibilities are endless. It is important to share some positive thoughts that make both of you look forward to the future. This will help make the process of passing time faster.

#2: We agree regarding frequency of contact

If you live hundreds or thousands of miles from each other it's common to feel separated. Long-distance relationships that work require regular interactions and sharing (the "relationship" with each other part). Texting, phone, email postal mail, webcams... You should make use of them all. Be aware that there is a hierarchy of benefits to these communications systems. The best option is to utilize the webcam and an online phone such as Skype in order that you can both see and communicate with one another. Emails and texts are excellent for small notes, but not more than that since they're so prone to interpretation. Be sure to send presents photographs, pictures, home film clips, and classic love letters by post also. There's nothing more satisfying than receiving a present from a loved one who is far away and it will let your partner know how much you cherish you and that you are thinking of them.

It's now more convenient than ever before to stay connected over long distances. Just a few texts, emails and phone calls every day at least per day (or even every week) make you feel like being completely involved in one another's lives. Your relationship's success relies on your being connected, so schedule uninterrupted time in order to "catch up" with each other's lives.

If the other person is unable to get time to engage in even 10 minute conversation, yet has the time to hang out with friends, attend an event, go to for a workout, cook, or even rest, you have an idea that this person isn't as into you in the way you believe. If the person you are talking to is really keen on you, they'll exhibit all the evidence that they don't just want to maintain the relationship, but also want to be closer. If he or she truly loves you, then s/he'll not just make time for you, but also make talking to you the most important thing on his/her schedule of tasks to accomplish. However, you should be realistic and don't be a slave to their time as you're overflowing with desire.

You'll be away from each other for some period of time, and you'll need to keep contact... however, how often? Can you communicate with your partner frequently even though you're not able to be there for them? It is, in fact, possible. Although it's true that living far from your partner can be challenging, think about how often you'd contact them if they were in the same town as you. If it's only about once or twice a week, you shouldn't be calling them on a daily basis since it's unnatural and can make things uncomfortable. Also, you don't want to make it a habit to call your partner on a regular basis. If you've had an unsatisfactory morning at work, and are not in a good mood Don't try to insist on an exchange. Also, don't ignore the old saying that "absence causes the heart to become more affectionate". Make use of the distance between you to keep things interesting and keep you eager to hear the voice of your soulmate or to read their emails.

Talking and writing are great ways to connect with your spouse. There is nothing that warms your heart more than receiving a hug or hearing the voice of your partner. But it's not like gazing into the eyes of your partner. Therefore, invest in an online camera, and give the extra dimension to your long distance relationship. Even if it's just for a short time having a face-to face conversation with the special person that you love keeps things fresh and alive. Also, invest in a high-quality webcam. You need to be able see the images clearly and loudly.

Make use of this one liner in your favor. What is a one-liner? It's a good question. In the context of relationships that are long distance It's not a joke or a jolly note to your spouse that will make them feel wonderful. The message should be brief and sweet, but also meaningful. If you want your one-liner to be effective it must be text-based (a phone call isn't going to be effective) and you can either you can send it by email or text to your beloved. Do it now - it's as simple to do. Send, for instance, an easy "I really love you" or "I am missing you" or "Just watched our favorite show and was thinking of the person you love!". The goal will be to catch your loved one by surprise and give the warm feeling of a hug to their hearts. It's very effective and is among the most effective methods to spice up your long-distance romance.

#3 Ideas for romantic ideas for relationships that span a long distance

How do you remain in love with someone you've never met? Romance is based on thoughtfulness creativeness, sharing feelings of love and intimacy. There are many ways to show your romantic side, no matter how close you may be. What is most important to your partner is the feeling that they are loved and that you're considering them in spite of the many distractions in life where you're. Keep them in your thoughts by committing to maintain regular contact. Send them thoughtful and romantic love packages, as you have discussed via mail. Make time for your own time on your internet cam phone gatherings. The most intimate things you can do to create successful long distance relationships is to think about for the next chapter of your life together. Talk about what you're planning to do in the coming years. Always make sure to mention how much you look to spending time with them physically and living a life together. Think about what you're going to do the moment you meet the next time. Also, make use of all your fond memories and shared memories. Discussing the activities you've taken part in and plan to do is a great method to keep the spark flowing in any relationship. Make sure you give your partner frequent and regular affirmations of your love and dedication. Be aware of any miscommunications and try to establish the clarity you need in your interactions with your long distance partner. It is important to ensure that when you are using the phone or web camera that you are not with anyone else. So you can be more expressive and there'll be nothing to distract you.

Don't overlook special occasions when you're spending a long period of time without your partner, it's very easy to lose the "relationship" aspect of your life. You can get into a more "me-centric" mentality. Although this is normal but it's not something you can be able to accept. It is important to preserve the small pleasures that come from being around someone in their lives One way to achieve this is to keep a record of special events. Don't forget birthdays, and the anniversaries. Also, don't forget any minor events that can be significant to your spouse. If you're not sure, make reminders in your calendar. When it's time, you can give your partner a sweet note that can bring joy to their faces.

4. Keep the feeling of romance and fun alive

The most challenging aspects of long-distance relationships is that you aren't able to reach out to your woman and tell them "let's take a stroll at the park" or visit and invite them to join you to drinks. If you don't have these small moments of shared time that people who are in close relationships consider to be normal It's not uncommon for two individuals to get trapped in the waiting and future that they totally forget about what's happening now. The relationship gradually gets less exciting and eventually goes away.

To prevent this from happening, try to have "virtual date nights". You can, for instance, plan to go to the cinema to see the latest film on the same date and afterwards, call each other to talk about thoughts, experiences and ideas. If you can get a time zone that works and it's affordable, rent a film and then watch the film "together" with someone else over the phone. You could also play card games or games on the internet, for instance. Don't not forget to flirt, seduce and let him or her know what a huge amount he or she means to you as well as how deeply you cherish them or them. It is important to take the appropriate steps to keep your sense of enjoyment, shared interests romantic love and passion.

5. Make Your spouse feel special

Being lonely is a certainty in a relationship that is long distance. If you're truly in love with another person, you can't not feel lonely. When you're at your most solitudes, you have to find a way to create something positive for your partner. It could be anything from sending an email or a message to placing an order for something to be delivered. Make them feel like you care by making them feel as happy that you possibly can. Chances are that they're being lonely and sad and you can pick them up by giving them a unique present.

Take a moment to think about what you feel about yourself and what you would prefer to feel treated by your spouse Do that for them. It's a fantastic method to let them know that you're always thinking of your partner and that you will never forget about them.

#6 The art of coping with sexual aversion and attraction

If you're healthy, you're likely to get a little sexy, and it's difficult to find satisfaction if you're with someone on located on the other side of the country or even the globe. It is vital that you both are in agreement about the boundaries of your relationship. Some people are comfortable with the notion of their partners having other relationships even when they're not together. However, most people don't.

Find out what your relationship is and the degree of commitment you're willing to offer to each one another. Evaluate the potential for temptation. If your partner is going off to university in the West Coast while you are going to school at the East Coast, you have to assess how strong your bond is since you both will confront a lot of temptation through others right in front of you. Each couple is different and only you and your partner will be able to decide if you are able to be able to commit. The trick is to keep your communication channels and add plenty of times for intimate, high-tech sex the form of phone sex or webcam sexual relations. You must have the trust of your partner within a relationship for this, since you do not want to discover that your loved one has uploaded your naked images on the internet! Effective long distance relationships provide for sexual resentment by scheduling "fun" time. They also focus on the sensation of intimacy and deepness and this is a part of all the communication you make. The more you share your authentic self, the more intimate your relationship will become. In terms of overcoming the temptations This is the time to put your faith into play as well as your future plans you plan. The majority of people can survive just by relying on the hot things! Be sure to carry through what you've said you'll give each other whenever you get together!

7: Overcoming fears anxiety and fear of cheating

Every romantic relationship can be characterized by anxiety and fear about cheating However, generally, long-distance relationships are more difficult to deal with those emotions. The grass always appears greener on the other hand especially when one person has been away to somewhere exciting while the other stays at home. If every time you speak to your loved one, there seems to be a celebration going on within the backdrop, it's no surprise that you are feeling betrayed. The most important thing is not to get yourself into a bind over it. It's normal to feel anxious and a bit unsure. It's going to happen at some point, so take it as it comes and don't allow it to escalate. Keep your confidence in yourself and confidence in yourself. Do the things you love doing. You're a valuable attractive, fascinating, and attractive person. It's essential for your mental well-being to take the view that your spouse is fortunate to have you as a part of their lives. You should think that you're the ideal option for them. Effective long-distance relationships utilize the distance to gain a better perception of the relationship. Recognize that you can build an effective connection with any number of individuals. However, you've decided to form a strong connection with someone who happens to be a considerable distance away from you at the moment. From this perspective, your relationship will always be based on a choice. When you decide to form an intimate relationship, rather than it being based on neediness or a desire to believe that it is the only thing that matters and only.

Distance is a method to play with anxiety and fear of the unknown. You are so envious of someone that you begin to think about cheating on you , even though you are sure that they are not the kind of cheater. Even though he/she has given you no reason to believe that he/she could be cheating or cheat, you tell yourself "You don't know" and "Don't be fooled!"

If you're not willing to be able to trust your partner or woman, you are not in need to be in a long-distance relationship since in LDRs trust is the most important thing. If you don't trust someone, there's nothing to gain from the relationship. Without trust, maintaining an extended relationship is unattainable.

Talk about your fears and anxiety with them and, once you've received the confidence you require Let it go. If s/he is looking to cheat, they will and there's no way to stop it. Relax your mind and focus on establishing solid foundations to your relationships. It's also beneficial to do your best to be reliable, to perform what you say you're going to do, and to demonstrate you're reliable. The trust factor is both positive and negative!

#8 How to deal with doubts about your feelings

Accept the fact that it's normal for your passion to decrease occasionally. Every relationship is prone to fluctuation and change and you shouldn't interpret this as an indication of a failed relationship. Don't be afraid to voice your feelings in a way that is secure. If you've planned your relationship well you'll have prepared for the eventuality, and you'll both understand that it's an inevitable part of being separated. Review where you are now and where you're headed in your relationship. Be sure you have goals in your relationship to strive for and are regularly discussing the next meeting you have and any plans for the future. People who are constantly focused on the present can have a difficult time staying in contact with their feelings for people when they're not with them. If this is the case ensure that both the person you are with realize that you may not be as expressive when you are away. If this is the case it is recommended to schedule regular meetings, if you can. It is equally important for your personal life, not just for your relationship, to gain a more complete and longer-term view of time. The most successful individuals financially are those who make plans for 10 20-30 years, 20-30 years in advance. Similar is the case with relationships. Long-distance relationships that are successful happen when both parties view the distance as being temporary and with a fixed time frame, and are working towards a future together.

#9: Relationships that work at close proximity and distance

You'll eventually want to find the best way to be with someone else and to build a happy relationship.

Chapter 11: Realism About The Next Step

More than 50 percent of long distance relationships have ended. The number of marriages that are long distance are on the rise in the past couple of decades. The rapid growth of internet-based dating websites in the last decade is also the reason for why relationships between people who live far apart are increasing. Keep in mind, however, the fact that just 64% the matches are due to the sameness of appearance and compatibility. Therefore, you need to work on your skills to create an enjoyable and loving relationship. Through the internet, you can create real connections with people , even if they reside on the other part of the globe. Your neighbor may be involved in a long distance relationship, or your colleague could be in a long-distance relationship, and even your CEO may be part of one. You're not alone. If you have colleagues, friends and family members engaged in a long distance relationship. Discuss it with them. You might be amazed by their perspective regarding their relationship. If you as well as your partner are able to adjust to changes that take place in your relationship , you'll be able to enjoy a satisfying relationship even distance.

I've entered a lot of long-distance relationships believing that this individual will be the one that I get married to simply because I'm convinced that the final purpose of any relationship you're entering is marriage. It's the way I was educated. However, in previous relationships after years or months of visits, talking or visits, and finding out lots about each other, we find out that we're not compatible or we're not able to handle the distance that we have to travel before breaking into. As I say, such is the way of life for me and my former ex-lovers were never meant to become a couple. That's one of the reasons for breakup, the falling apart, and the feeling of being helpless. This allows you to find another person, whether it's your closest friend or someone who lives three thousand miles away.

When you and your spouse begin to drift, for one reason or another Be honest about how you feeling. If you're feeling that you're not getting along anymore, be honest and do not lead your partner to the other side. It isn't a good idea for both of you to be in the long-distance relationship to believe that everything is okay but it's not. In my opinion, breaking the ice in a long-distance relationship is like obtaining an guilty plea in a court proceeding where you're not present. What can you do to protect yourself from being sucked into a breaking up over the phone or via text message or via video call. What I can tell you from my personal experience is that if you convince or beg your partner to remain with you, then they are the perfect relationship for the right person. If your partner isn't loving and devoted to you, don't try to convince them for love if your partner is determined to break up the relationship. This applies to any relationship.

Know that some of your close family and friends you may try to convince you to leave the relationship since they aren't aware of the aspects of a long-distance relationship. They may try to convince you into separating from your spouse and moving on since they don't understand how you could have the same future with someone who is located far from you. If you truly cherish your partner, then you could tell your critics how confident and serious your relationship. I personally don't enjoy negativity from people who criticize my relationship, therefore I resent those who say my relationship will not work out because my girlfriend is distant. That's why having conversations about the future boost confidence in the strength of your long-distance relationship. I am confident in the love I share in my relationship and don't have to explain to people who are skeptical why I'm in my long-distance relationship. It's really not their business , and they're able to continue to move forward.

If you are feeling like you're in need of a break, talk with your partner about having a brief break. Make it clear the reason for this break that it isn't an end of the line and provide reasons for the reasons why this break is beneficial to your relationship. Also, consider your partner's perspective regarding the matter. If you or your spouse are drawn to seeing different people while in a relationship, both partners must consider each other's opinions and find the best solution for both of both of you.

Sometimes, you require your own space, even in a relationship, where you're sharing lots of physical space from your loved one. You should take time for your goals, the ones you've set for yourself in whole, relationships can get tiring because you're more focused on your partner instead of on you. Some people are not able to handle the stress of a relationship that is not working. do not stay in a relationship when you aren't willing to commit the heart, soul and energy. This isn't fair for your partner in any way.

Remember that not all relationships are will be able to work. First foremost, be content.

Chapter 12: Problems

"A problem can only be a hurdle when you bow before it."

Every relationship has obstacles to be tested by the degree to which you cherish your spouse. Unexpected challenges can come up and you have to take it on. You need to be tough enough and inspire your spouse with positivity to ensure that you can overcome any obstacle that may arise in your relationship.

TIME

One of the most frequent problems in an extended relationship is time. Your partner or you requires more time. The issue of time is also because either of you or your partner is not able to provide enough time to both of you. There are other reasons why either of you have changed over time and are now putting in only a little effort.

It is as crucial to have time as the effort. It is essential to always make time for your partner , and even make time for the two of you to get together. It's common for each of you to request time because you're apart. A lot of times, you don't get to spend time with your partner, and it can get into the way of staying loyal to your partner.

SUBSTANCES

Being too cautious about the actions your partner doing, or even the people you are having conversations with is a problem that can cause disputes over trust and constant fighting. You don't have to be aware of every detail since your partner could believe that you don't trust them.

There will always be the person who seems to be a threat to your relationship. Your partner may hang out frequently with this specific person and they may be close , but that does not mean that your partner is behaving badly towards you. Sometimes, your partner simply requires someone to spend time with.

THE EXCITEMENT A PARTICIPANT

Here's another thing you ought to pay attention to.

Did you notice how perfect everything was in the initial few months you were together? It's because you're still trying to figure things out and your partner remains an unknown to you. The first time you meet, everything is flawless but as time passes it gets dull and sometimes a bit boring.

The majority of long distance relationships end due to the fact that either the person you are with or your partner went out of the intimacy with your partner. It becomes routine, and eventually you are familiar routines that you've done. Nothing seems to engage two of you and the of you become bored. It's not really working and you need something to be energized once more.

COMMUNICATION

A long distance relationship requires both of you and your partner to be in contact throughout the day. Most problems occur due to the fact that you don't remember to call or even send a text message to your partner. You did not notify them of your changes or update them about your plans. Then, you have a miscommunication and begin fighting and the most likely, you split the relationship.

Communication is a crucial aspect in a long distance relationship as it's the line you share to your partner. It helps strengthen your relationship. Your partner is dependent on your attention at all times particularly when he or she is down, which is why it's important to be in a constant communication to your spouse.

They are the driving forces that make each relationship successful. When problems arise, it indicates that your relationship requires improvements or to address the issues that led to the problem. The problem is not as severe as they might seem. Problems help us improve and allow us to come up with solutions. The relationship is able to grow more enduring.

If issues arise, you must be prepared to lay your pride aside and admit the facts. Sometimes, it is necessary be humble, and apologize even if it's not your responsibility. Being kind and patient with your partner can reduce the likelihood of breakups. Don't ever let your emotions affect your decisions.

Problems are not an indication of breaking up.

Chapter 13: Plan, Talk And Talk About Share

If you are in an extended relationship, in order to make it truly work it is essential that both partners are dedicated to filling the gap that distance can create with significant components. If you're not able to physically meet, the next best option is to communicate to a deeper level. To do this effectively, you must to constantly plan, communicate and communicate with one another as frequently as you are able to.

MAKING PLANS

Even though you're separated does not mean that you cannot make decisions and plans together. It's vital to keep this aspect of your relationship as it can do wonders to bring a sense of calm even when you're not at the same level. If it's not about things which you're not doing together it demonstrates a lot of teamwork. It also helps you remain involved in one another's lives in a more active manner. Even something as simple as selecting an outfit or deciding the food you'll have to eat at dinner will leave you feeling more in touch. If these small choices are made a habit, it opens the an opportunity to plan out bigger and more ambitious plans in a calm and secure way. It becomes clear the way you solve problems and the steps that you follow to take decisions and plan your plans for the future.

You'll notice that you always be able to count on one another when you need to make crucial, life-changing decisions that will certainly strengthen your relationship. There will be a sense that you appreciate your partner's opinions and input when making these kinds of major decisions.

Discussing emotions

We've put a lot of importance on how crucial communicating through either video chats or talking on the phone , rather than texting to ensure that you're in a position to accurately express how you're feeling. If you only communicate via text messages, you are at risk of getting your words or tone incorrectly interpreted. This could result in a massive gap in communications.

The thing you'll need to do in your long-distance relationship is being aware of the kind of conversations that you and your partner are having. It is important to take care not to let distance limit you in expressing your love and emotions generally. You must be able to show vulnerability and always be sincere and compassionate. It's crucial to understand that your words won't only be a means of communicating through regular conversations, but they'll have a bigger impact in substituting your physical affection for your partner. Instead of a kiss, a hug or holding hands, you must to make sure that you show your partner love with kind words and affection to ensure that the passion and heat do not fade away or fizzle out.

Sharing your thoughts with each other will also increase your trust and strengthens your relationship since you'll become best friends and you are aware that this is the person you'd like to share your secrets and feelings with. You'd like to communicate with your partner even when things aren't getting the best of you or you're concerned or anxious about something.

Experiences with sharing

The other thing that goes along with sharing your hopes and feelings is of course sharing your own experiences. Nothing can help to bridge the gap between you like putting together the story of your experience with your companion. Discuss events that occurred during each day. Discuss how it impacted your life, share photos and create videos. The use of visual aids makes an event seem more clearand makes them feel like they're right in the same place with you.

The ability to structure your communications in a relationship that is long distance will allow it to grow exponentially and allow you to traverse long distances and distances in an relaxing manner. Utilizing these suggestions will cover every aspect you require to cover so that the two of you do not have to be weighed down by the fact that you're separated from one another. It can ease the pressure of not having the ability to see or touch each other face-to-face, as you'll be compensating by providing stability and structure and a future outlook that give you a sense of security. Through sharing your emotions with your words, and sharing your photos by sharing your experiences, you're giving your partner the chance to look at the world with your eyes, and also the green light to receive your complete attention and affection and makes distance insignificant for the majority of the time and it's worthwhile.

Chapter 14: Reconnecting With An Extensive Distance Lover

After breaking up over long distances, getting back together with your ex could seem a bit hopeless. You've certainly attempted to reconnect but it's not the same as it was before.

As if keeping an ongoing relationship over a long period of time was not enough, now you're trying to determine if regaining the spark that once captivated you is feasible from the place you're. In the majority of cases it's better to leave However, if you're determined to get back the affections of your ex-love There are some ways to change the odds in your favor.

However, before you embark on extravagant romantic plans You must be prepared to deal with the drama that could befall you. If you ended your relationship with a bad attitude prepare for the problems that remain unresolved to surface. However much you desire a new beginning there will be a need to face the past in at some point or another, so be ready to experience all the tension again.

Reuniting with an ex-partner from a distance relationship can be difficult as reconciliations require three key elements for successful: Communication sincerity, sincerity, and physical contact. It's possible to overcome your sincerity and communication issues, but making contact with your ex physically could be challenging especially if you'll have travel to another country to meet your ex once more. What do you do in this scenario?

Establish communication

In the process of trying to win the ex back, communication is a crucial factor. It's impossible to maintain a good relationship without communication. If you've had a bad experience on this front before, you may need to resolve some issues with yourself before attempting to open conversations between you and your partner. Do not be too cocky in this moment. You must be open about the actions you've committed that could have caused a breakdown in communication within the relationship. Then you will be able to speak for your partner.

If you're looking to reach for your ex ensure that you don't put the person off by being all at once. Choose a neutral and comfortable medium that isn't overly intrusive. Instead of calling to make a call, what better way to test your luck via email or private messaging? This allows your ex to decide if would like to reply with your email. Making a phone call could put your ex in the edge of a bind.

Be sincere

If you believe that your ex-partner is happy to communicate with them again then the following step would be to demonstrate your sincerity. Accept your apology in order to get by reestablishing friendship. Be careful not to rush the ball to be lovers. Do not rush through this phase of reconciliation as it may be the most crucial. Spend the time necessary to feel comfortable with one the other once more. If you're dealing with unresolved issues you have to address, now is the best time to go through the issue. If your partner will talk about the issue. If your ex-partner says they're not willing to discuss the issue at this point do not dwell on it for too long. It is important to allow your partner time to process the situation independently. Don't overly insist on putting labels on the two of you. Keep in touch for the length of time your ex would like. Consider yourself fortunate to have another chance.

Make sure you are there

Being physically present may be difficult at the moment however that shouldn't deter you from going. You can show that you love by sending small tokens, and being accessible to your ex via phone calls or chats. It's possible that you are eager to win over your ex-partner however, don't get excited about it. Do not always be the first person to start a conversations or send messages. You should be aware that your ex-partner can reach you at any time, but never until you've become their stalker. Give your relationship the enough time to develop independently. Contact via physical means may not be feasible but that doesn't mean it gives you the right to send your lover multiple messages daily. At the very least, you should maintain some dignity.

Chapter 15: Tips And Tricks For Making Your Love One Love You And Want To Be With You Even While He/She Is Absent.

Be unique, be imaginative in your thinking, be innovative, and talk to your loved ones. Discuss ideas, imagine the future together, come up with fun plans and goals that you can look forward to, so the time goes by faster. Create plans for events once you are back together, and that are not bound by anything. Make it clear to the person you are with that you are a couple and not only in the short-term relationships. So, both of you would be more inclined to keep your relationship. Be dependable to your partner, make certain to have each other's support and help no matter what steps they take to improve or doing something else. Have fun, laugh and laugh with each other Most people aren't willing to acknowledge how much they love the way you smile or the way that you style your hair. It's the little things that makes you feel loved by somebody. It's in the manner in which they walk, talk or laugh, sometimes even the way they gaze at you with the desire to hold their love for you. Love is hidden in every small and insignificant things at first glance, but when you consider it, they're the things that you most miss when you are used to seeing them.

The overall quality of relationships may be great but once insignificant arguments or patterns begin to pile up and get within the people, they will be prone to becoming angry and, at times, resentful by the person who is next to them. The most frustrating part is that it's a matter of time and it's hard to know exactly the time and place. You fall asleep feeling happy and in love, only to find that you wake up completely confused and sour about the whole relationship with the one person. A person is only able to handle an inordinate amount of unresolved issues before becoming distant and distant.

My best suggestion I could provide is to solve any issue... not even the most insignificant bit of information or behavior that irritates you, discuss about it. Change. Evolve. Do not keep it in a closed-off place it's a dangerous path towards self-destructing and depression. Let everything out. Communication is the most important thing! Remind them of what they mean to you , or how much they mean to you. The proof is always in the actions, not in words. Let them see and impress them through every little bit. Be yourself in the most positive way you can, and continue to surprise and pleasing them. Do not let fears or doubts interfere with your success (no regardless of your or their side). Discuss everything on a every day basis. Whatever way satisfied people are with their partners , there is always a little things that are left unattended and rarely discussed, which will later turn into disputes that can be that are unpleasant for both parties.

Name your pets together Be creative, adorable innocent and playful. Nothing makes an evening for your loved ones other than a smile from you. A text, phone call or a note, which shows how much they are to you and how much you love them. It's also a sign that they're the first thing to pop up into your head every morning and last you think of at night.

Give each other small gifts and remind each other that you both love one another and that you never forget things like anniversaries birthdays, cute details about dates and fun stories about the activities you've enjoyed together.

Don't be too close to them. You don't want to frighten them away or bore them with your constant nagging, and the desire to have all their time. Let them have space, but don't make them feel lonely or unimportant. Make sure to keep your conversations at the middle of the rainbow do not bore them, but at the same do not let them feel lonely or unimportant.

Don't make them feel like they're you're not there. Nobody says you have to be at your toes, but don't let them feel like they're in a state of worry. In the event that you're out with your friends, but staying in the evening could cause a fight, or cause problems for the future growth or your relationships. Engage them in conversation, assure that they are safe and give them the sense of being in control.. particularly when you're not there.

Make them feel as close to your home as is possible. Give a little information about your loved ones' lives and family drama. Be like your children, be amazed by everything in life. Have fun, and overcome the distance.

While you're away, you shouldn't wish for the spark and desire to go off into the distance So you must keep them engaged. Speak naughty things to one another, and believe it or not , it's the most important factor in keeping couples close. If this desire fades in a relationship that is young It's not good to be without a sexual desire towards each other. It's the only way of permitting you to show your love for each other and release a massive amounts of stress and tension.

Chapter 16: Skype And Facetime

It is important to create with your partner since you'll have to download the program onto your smartphone or tablet to ensure that you're connected to each other prior to your partner departing to travel. This means downloading the software creating your account, and adding your loved one to contacts. Skype requires a little bit the majority of Internet time, which is why it is also necessary to be on a plan for your phone which includes a decent amount of Internet connectivity.

Facetime is, on the other hand is slightly more user-friendly, but you'll need to enter the number of your loved ones and verify that it is working prior to the time that they disappear. If you aren't happy with the way you view at these apps, put the phone at a short distance away, and then balance it against books or some other object in order to be within a reasonable distance, and that the phone isn't moving even when you're talking because this could be very frustrating.

There are additional apps that can help you with this. If, for instance, you are on Facebook then you are able to include photos on a regular basis in order to ensure that your dear ones informed of what you're doing. Facebook is useful too since in the messenger app you can communicate with your loved ones via video chat if you wish to. If you are aware that you will be separated and you want to set this up ahead of time is a good option. Another application that could aid you in reducing phone bills is WhatsApp since it allows direct calls to numbers that your phone can't call for free.

I utilize WhatsApp to communicate with people using mobile phones that aren't included in my internet service and that's what I love about it. It isn't a matter of where you live. You can reach them via text message, phone call or video.

In the present day it's important to get everything planned out in advance and to have tested and tried it. If you're involved in an Internet relationship but haven't had the chance to meet your partner on the ground, apps like these apps eliminate a lot doubts since you are able to view your loved ones in real-time. Perhaps you've exchanged messages and may think your beloved is in the same boat as you, however when you see them in person you may be surprised to find that their actions and appearances are not what you imagined, which is why it's a good idea, in a sense, to utilize apps such as this to ensure that you are aware of precisely what you're getting yourself into.

A word of caution

If your relationship is long distance and is with someone you do not have a relationship with, keep off sending intimate photos of body parts. They could end up on the internet and could be embarrassing to your future self. Begin by getting to know the person first, and make use of the tools that are available to share your company, but don't introduce that type of intimacy until you've actually had a conversation and built trust with each other. It's very easy for people who are vulnerable to believe that a long distance relationships are real however they're being played by people who like playing with their emotions.

If you're in a long-distance relationship with a stranger from a different country, ensure that you connect through Skype or Facetime when you can so that you are aware of who this person is and not the person whose emails claim they are. You might believe that based on the conversations you've exchanged that you're exceptional because it's easier to record your emotions than to express them, particularly when you're at the computer and on your own. The most important aspect of a long-distance relationship with any person is Honesty. It is the basis of good relationships. If you are doubtful about whether or not it's going to work make sure you voice them and talk about the issues. Do not appear to be an individual you're not, as if the relationship is to last it will depend on your authenticity completely.

As you'll find out during the following chapter, being honest is an important part to play when you're not with your loved ones due to work. I'd like to remind you that a long-distance relationship is not a success without the courage to be honest with your partner. Doubting whether the relationship will be successful will hurt feelings, but more so when you're not from the person you love.

Chapter 17: Always Maintain The Right Attitude, Think Positive, Don't Be Jealous And You'll Be Content

A positive attitude towards those who are more likely to get into an argument or to remain calm about their emotions by tucking them away until they explode on the wrong person's doorstep is essential in order to be content with anyone.

Don't be jealous, put your confidence in your spouse. You don't want to end up over-protecting them or constantly expressing doubt in their actions. If it's designed to be it is. Love and relationship are two things that aren't meant to be forced or pressured into getting in a particular shape.

No matter what the distance between people isn't an assurance that your partner will always be honest and loving. If someone chooses to hide your secret from you they don't need to be away from you to perform it. He could be lying in bed close to you and commit it at night. It's entirely up to a person to decide if they'll behave in sincerity towards you.

Make sure you can endure the distance. It's well-known that distance is the most significant obstacle you can face in the course of a relationship. It's about refining the motives of a couple. If you are able to endure the distance between you, you are probably meant to remain together for the rest of your lives. Your bond is irreparable It is safe to say that nothing can harm it in the future.

Chapter 18: The Visits

You might think that you have to go out frequently and I certainly do. But the statistics will prove that it will not determine your success or failure. You will definitely be sad to see that person, hugging them, holding them, and gazing into their eyes. The importance of intimacy is that when you are in a relationship that is long distance you develop by different means. Long Distance can lead to a gradual and steady growth, and a more mature relationship in which you can talk and growing in deeper areas is possible because you have to communicate in a different way and deeper than the local relationship.

So, each week, once every month, or even every 6 months, take advantage of that time to let yourself develop in different ways.

Utilize the tools that are that are available to you. There's a wide range of tools that are available for you to use. There are some that are fun, while some are more serious in the realm of connecting.

As we look at the numbers in this book you'll discover that the things you hear about and what's actually true regarding Long Distance Relationships are totally different. I was also surprised. You'll see what I mean in just a couple of pages.

The thing about visiting is that you're likely need to be there for one another in times of need. There will occasions when you'll have to travel and help your loved ones as a sacrifice. it's a part of the field of Long Distance Relationships. In times of stress, you're going to be required to give your support to the very best of your ability , and go above and over and above. Do you think it would be easy to leave, pick up the phone and not fret about it? That's not love. Love cares and is present in good and bad times. Be aware that you have to be there for your loved one.

Venting is also a typical element in relationships, you will likely take a call or look over an email that can be sometimes explosive. It could be a difficult morning at work or dealing with the X or your kids, but I guarantee it will take place and you need to be attentive and take it in stride. My son and I are aware that the bad days will come but sometimes it's not our fault. However, there are times when we need to hear a little correction in the direction of love, care, and a pat on the back if we aren't understanding the message.

Sometimes, you need to vent! We are all venting together and that's a great thing you're not able to hide the bad times you've had with your man I suppose you can, but really, how do you go about creating a bond? Remember that relationships are not without poor days and good days, and good days. Take advantage of every day together and expand by leaps and leaps and.

My boyfriend along with me have served as listening to boards to one another. We simply listen to one another work through the day or express our get frustrated. It is helpful to listen, and also helps let it all out.

Take care This isn't about a negative discussion that always occurs to me, my friend. It's your responsibility to confront this or get away from it. I'm talking about those times You know, well here's an illustration.

I awoke each day to an enormous sink overflowing with dishes cake crumbs scattered in the kitchen counter trash leaking into the garbage bag, which was meant be removed, tables and chairs which were to be taken to the basement. When I moved them , the towel I cleaned were dumped in the corner. I tried for a shower and put on an old towel to clean my hands, and it was filled with whiskers on the chin. To finish it off, I got to work and I spilled my tea all across the front of the car.

Yes, it's an extremely stressful day.

BE POSITIVE

The first and most important thing to do is never talk to anyone about your relationship whether long distance or locally. OKAY! This must be said in the open here.

It is your relationship and nobody knows more than you do. Be respectful and thank them whatever advice they wish to offer or tell you an account of a friend who dated the man for four states and then tell them to not thank you! I'm not interested in hearing the story, but if you require that advice, I'll know where to go.

I'm not sure where the rumors began however from what I've seen and my reading, I've learned that relationships with long distances won't be successful. Some people will use someone they know to support the statistics they've read about, however I am here to say that this isn't true. In the last paragraph are facts that will demonstrate what I'm talking about. I won't lie to you I'm sure of it!

There will moments when you're likely to feel down and feel lonely It's inevitable and you're going to have to summon the courage to get through those moments and remain in the best mood you possibly can. In those moments when you feel vulnerable , you can text your loved ones and tell them what you're feeling and maybe create a code word that signifies that you need some encouragement to push through.

Keep a notepad of positive thoughts or events that have transpired to remember the great moments you experienced and ones that you are planning for the near future.

I have a container that I keep, and I store everything in it. I have postcards from the places we went to and small things he might have left. I have matchbooks of places we dined. I enjoy looking through it, and it keeps me smiling while I recall the great times we've enjoyed together.

PLANN A FUTURE TOGETHER

The process of planning for the future can be fun , and keeping the idea that you are in the in your head that things will and could change can help ease the stress of the planning. Planning is enjoyable even during the day, it's similar to dreaming with a goal If I am an author in the top 50 and when I go to Hawaii or when I am old again We all dream, and want.

I believe the best method to plan is to talk about your goals and dreams for the future What do you want to achieve and to be? where do you intend to be and where you want to go? All things are important and it should be discussed.

You must then establish a goal, a goal isn't a change with the flick of a penny or mood, it is something that you must achieve. The goal is to achieve it with your partner and you'll only know how to accomplish these goals, there's no rule that is set or time limit. simply have fun and create your life with each other and work toward your target.

My dream is to build a tiny home near the beach, that my children can visit to unwind and relax while the husband (yep I did say that term) along with me are able to sit back and relax. I want it to be cozy and spacious and, most importantly, I'm looking for those times.

Recently , my friend and I sat down together and made a list of the five states we'd prefer to reside in and of those five states, we had three commonalities. We then looked over cities as well as some details on City-Data.com and picked the location which we would like to become our home. It was enjoyable creating our dream home and we have some things to work through before getting there, but we're already getting there.

We definitely took the path of least resistance, but this is what we do and we spent a lot of time talking and researching states and cities. I loved the fact that He was so enthralled and we now have this city that we might someday be able to call our home.

What works for you, plan your life with each other and discuss it? I can't emphasize it enough: talk!

Chapter 19: Stay In Contact Every Day

There are couples who have a huge distance between them due to work. For instance, Carl was forced to relocate into San Francisco to work at the 60k-per-year tech job to provide for his family, wife and children in Kansas. Carl is a long-hour worker, however he's fortunate enough to live in a place where the time zone difference isn't too bad which means he's able to have a good night with his children every night. Other people aren't as fortunate Take Mika or Andrew. Andrew has a home in New York and is a student at New York University. His girlfriend has not met his family as she lives in Osaka, Japan, They were introduced through Mixi the Japanese website where anyone can blog and connect on. Andrew cannot talk to Mika during the time he is asleep, or when he's awake. This is because, when Andrew is asleep, Mika is starting her day, and once Mika goes to go to bed, Andrew is brewing up coffee.

Whatever challenges you may face in keeping connected the most important thing in a long-distance relationship is to remain in contact every day.

Why?

It is possible to lose contact when you don't communicate regularly. There are no ifs, ends, or ifs. Life is ever-changing and if you've only got 10 minutes to talk to your loved one make sure you do it. Every day, we're getting to know new people as well as visiting new places and facing new issues. It's a known fact that you'll talk more with your girlfriend during the beginning of a relationship than at any other moment or of the whole relationship. Why? Because you're just beginning to feel love. When we are in love, our bodies are bombarded by endorphins that make us feel happy and content when we speak to our spouses. After you've finished the AIM chat, you feel nice, even a bit weird inside! Your day is brighter and you are more friendly at strangers. You show more kindness to people around you, you let doors open, you give your seat on the bus or train. You're happy.

The feeling of happiness is one which is always in need of being fed, strengthened and provided with food.

We are all fortunate to not lose the relationship with our loved ones over time, but it isn't the same with all of us. As time passes by, we'll be more busy in our lives and begin to neglect our relationships with our loved ones. It might not be you, but it could be him initially telling you "oh I'm supposed to leave earlier this morning because I have to be up early the next day". Then it could be her saying "I cannot write much today, I've got many things to finish". Then you'll be used to the lower degree of communication until you're only speaking every two days. If both of you have busy lives and work overtime it's okay and normal. But if nothing has changed between your lives, keep an eye on! Distance doesn't make hearts feel more cherished in relationships with long distances in fact, it separates you two further and further!

How to Stay in Touch:

Instant Messaging Instant Messaging - free (AIM, MSN Messenger, Google Chat). Apart from phone calls as well as video conversations, it's crucial to spend at least five minutes a day of contact with your loved one via this channel.

Email - Why is that? It's free and easy to use. Every day try to send one email. It doesn't need to be a lengthy sentence about why you cherish the person you're writing to, just a brief phrase about how much they are important to you is sufficient. It is also possible to send them a hyperlink to a website that you've just viewed and enjoyed or a blog that you find interesting. The goal is to increase interactions.

Phone calls - This could be costly. If you don't have a plan for calling that allows international calls, this could cost you a hefty sum. A way to cut costs is to use the Internet line and make use of Google

Voice. It costs a flat amount per minute. I would suggest at least a 5 minutes phone call each week, at a minimum. If you reside in the USA there's a company named Unlimited Recharge. In the case of Unlimited Recharge you dial an American number and then the international number. You deposit money into your phone, and it is permanently linked to the number you dial. The UK version is called Rebtel. The advantage they have in comparison to Google Voice is that you can talk to your loved ones anywhere you go, since it's tied to your phone number. It's likely that I sound like an advertisement today, but the main point is that you have choices.

Quick Tip! Do you want to hear the voice of your spouse? Be sure to make phone calls important. Do not call someone just to ask "So what's up today?" It will eventually become annoying to those on the other phone. This is the reason why making a single phone call per day can be pleasant and memorable.

Video Chat - Now you can video chat with Google Chat, and any Mac computer has its standard iChat which supports video. Skype is another example of a no-cost Video chat program. They are all reliable and I would recommend a video chat at least once a week.

Personal Letters: After several months in an intimate relationship, you need to be aware of your partner's physical address. Let them know that you're planning compose a romantic letter and follow through it. It's romantic and lovely to look at the actual handwriting of the person you love dearly. Additionally, it's a great method of confirming whether you're being duped by your partner. If you're in high school and your boyfriend is in Australia is living with parents it's normal. But, if you've had a relationship with a man for a long time and you're both in your mid 20's and he's not willing to give your address due to the fact that the guy is "not yet ready" at the moment, beware! He could be married or in a relationship with another woman. If he is in love with you and has been with you for more than one year, there's any reason to believe that he would not want to share his address. NONE! If he's reluctant to talk to you, ask him that he is reluctant. Also , if he provides you with a an address that is a P.O. address (a box that is rentable from the postal office) inquire about the address of his actual residence. There is no reason to give you the address of a P.O. box rather than his real address, unless he's got something to cover up...

Always and I'm talking about always feeding your love

A relationship that is long-distance may require more commitment and love than a closer one. This is because, in the absence of our loved ones, we may be distracted by other people. Making new acquaintances can result in moments that your partner isn't missing out on. Your partner isn't there at the time you have an outdoor picnic with your friends, and you're not around while he's having a good time. If you both are in-the-house-all-the-time type, that's fine. However, you shouldn't be on all of the sites he's on You're not there to see the clothes she bought her or watching him write his movie reviews on IMDB.

Don't think that your relationship is going smoothly just because you're feeling well. If your spouse has a rough day, it's okay to just leave them alone however, if you notice the problem getting worse slow, you must discuss any issues. Even if everything is fine you should periodically ask "sweetie are you satisfied like me? What can I do to make you feel better?" with a smile. If you promote dialog, you will encourage dialogue that is constructive for a better relationship.

Put a date on your calendar!

Keep a time-line in your mind and then you'll get together (again).

There are three kinds of long-distance relationships:

First one I have never met in person but we are very connected on the internet.

Example: Your friend lives in Europe however you've not been to Europe You both chat daily on the internet.

Second type: We have met but are now living far away but are very close on the internet.

Example A: You met your boyfriend as you were instructing English to students in China. You've come back to your home in the United States but have no plans to travel to China between now and. Your boyfriend is currently is not able to travel to China or the United States, but you are online all day.

The Third Kind: have had experience and are able to meet difficulties.

Example: A partner is moving into South Carolina for school or to work. You reside within New York. You can ride for the Amtrak (long distance train) and visit him on weekends. You may be able to fly to the city on weekends! It's not possible to meet every weekend, however you'll try to squeeze in the weekend in per month in alternating rotations.

Or you both will remain in a long distance-relationship while in school but can see each other during spring break or when semester ends when one of the partners or both returns home.

Whatever type of relationship you're in it is important to keep an end-date in your mind. The date of the end is the day that you are living together. It doesn't have to happen today; it could be 20 years away. However, for a long-distance relationship to succeed, there needs to be some hope that the relationship will eventually evolve into an intimate relationship.

Perhaps it's the time your girlfriend receives her visa or you finally decide to experience what the city lights are But eventually, you have to feel a need, desire and desire to live with each other.

You can feed this date by:

1.) Discussing how wonderful it will be the day you have a chance to meet or have the opportunity to meet each day. If you truly love your partner and you want to be able to enjoy every right to visit him every day!

Therefore, talk about it. Discuss how you'd have breakfast on Sundays or watch an upcoming movie.

A QUICK TIP! Do you both enjoy films? What if you could go to a movie together now! If you are registered on Netflix account, then you are able to and agree to watch a movie togetherand then begin the film at the same point (say between 8pm and 6 pm his). You can also instant-message each other when you notice funny scenes in the film or discuss the film afterwards.

2.) Talking is great, but goals are what fuel our psyches and so it is important to agree on an date to end the relationship. The idea of ending dates can be a bit scary, particularly at the beginning of an affair (it contains the word "end" in it!), so don't push for a end-date if you just starting out. If it's been more than one year, you should start contemplating and planning the possibility of a date for an end. The date of the end does not mean either of you have to quit their jobs and relocate across the country or continents to live with the other. It's enough to have a simple meeting also. But it is important to set goals and keep you focused in a way that nothing else will.

Important End-date Questions:

1.) If it's a first time meeting:

Who will whom?

What is the best way to split the cost? (I suggest 50/50, unless one partner is struggling financially).

Where will the other party be staying? (Her home, in an hotel?)

2.) If you've met:

What is the future that we could live in harmony whether through unions, marriage, or living in close proximity to one another?

What can we do to achieve this?

These are difficult questions to talk about in relationship that is long distance, particularly since it is a matter of money.

But, they must be addressed in positive terms using positive phrases (use"we," or the word "we" in the majority of phrases like "I believe we ..."). Although discussing end-of-days is difficult, they are important because it provides you with something to look at in difficult times. It also helps keep you content in the relationship. While there are some people who are completely happy without having their partner around but we all crave and require physical affection. Computers can't substitute the feel of your girlfriend's hands, or your husband's gentle touch on your hair. Being able to smile and hug our loved ones makes us feel content. When relationships are in a rough patch we often be around people who have their partner nearby and begin to feel jealous, or frustrated with the distance relationship. This could be the case for teenage girls, older men or mature women. Choose a date to end the relationship and be faithful to it. You'll be happier.

What happens if your partner doesn't have a choice for an end date?

It's not always a big deal initially. It could be that he doesn't think about whether he's coming or is going to college or choosing a career path or your partner is in stuck between jobs. Some people cannot even think of what dishes they'd like to eat in a restaurant until they spot the waiter passing close by, and then are forced to choose a quick choice. You or your spouse likely to be one of those people and that's totally fine. But, if a year has passed and there's no date for an end, you'll need to be truthful to yourself and talk to your partner. If you've been in a relationship for five years and you are in need of a greater commitment, it's important to communicate the need with your spouse. Everyone doesn't want to get into a marriage that will end in a rut.

Quick tip! Make a plan for one date! Do you want to make it an upcoming weekend getaway or when that two-week vacation is scheduled? Make it a priority on both your calendars, and refer to it frequently. Knowing that the end of the week is approaching is sure to keep you motivated!

Chapter 20: Finding Balance

A equilibrium in your relationship is essential. Your life isn't made up entirely of time spent with your spouse. You're a whole being without your partner. Many people look to their spouse to shoulder the burden of their levels of happiness. However, this erroneous approach can cause you to be depend on the single most significant aspect of your life, your happiness. Take a look within yourself to discover the joy seed. It is important to nurture it. Grow it. Be aware that only you have the ability to make you content.

Your partner is a part of the quality of your life but is NOT part of the WHOLE life. He isn't. The pressure placed on someone else to provide you with that feeling of fulfillment and satisfaction is not right and is untrue. It's too much to ask from another person. Instead, look over your life and pinpoint the areas of your life that are most important towards your progress. It could be work as well as your hobbies, family and friends and, obviously, your relationship with your partner. Spend time in every aspect of your life that can improve your life.

Happiness-based people who are satisfied with their lives tend to be more enthusiastic in relationships. Be sure to excel in every aspect that matters to you. That is your job as well as your friends and your family. If you do not find ways to find that balance in your life then you'll be relying on your spouse for that which isn't his responsibility. If you've discovered the balance within your own life, you should look for it in your relationships as well as your job as well as other areas of your life.

For a test, create an inventory of aspects that make you a complete individual. This could include your friends, family and the location you live in and work in, your kids, partners and even your earnings. You can indicate your happiness in percent in front of every issue. For instance, you could consider that you're 70 percent satisfied at work 50 percent content with your family and 60% happy by your peers. Determine how each one of them affects your happiness and then figure out how you can make improvements in each one of them.

Chapter 21: The Long-Distance Relationship Recommendations

1. Set clear personal boundaries

The most important aspects of significant distance relationship advice is to set boundaries. "Above everything other things both of you must establish a few guidelines: what's worthy and what's not. worry about us explaining the limits that are associated with constancy are significant but for reasons that are not clear personal limits serve an enormous role in observing the other person from afar, as well. "Significant distance connections fail because of a lack of trust and a lack of space, no matter if it's just online space."

2. Make it appear as if you're single.

Absolutely. Apart from being in a relationship physically with a person else, experts claim that you can keep going in any way you like, kind similar to the time you were single.

Be proud of your life and celebrate your accomplishments. Upload photos and statuses on social media platforms about your life and how you've been doing. Spend time with your friends. Simply, create a mind-blowing maximum!

The more you are aware of and accept yourself, the better can focus on knowing and respecting your companion while you're together.

3. Do not spend more than three months apart

The most common question that anyone who is looking for a long-distance relationship advice seeks out is when you can stop to see your lover. It is best to do it as a clockwork base.

However, your timeline can alter depending on how you agree in your beliefs. This is to help you keep in mind why you like that person, in any event and also to have some sex. It also allows you to observe the way they grow personally.

4. Don't be a harpist all day

It's tempting to think that talking every and every day in an LDR is a requisite. Experts say that it's a little too much and could be detrimental in your friendship. There is no need to maintain constant communication. Keep a little of the secret!

In the event that you go for a few days without talking to your S.O. you'll have a more exciting conversation to look forward to within a few days. In addition, keeping an eye on another person and providing them with regular updates can be exhausting.

5. Don't solely rely on technology.

In the age of electronic gadgets, it is possible to connect even more deeply with your partner by segregating from snail mail. Try sending a note of love that includes a little of your favorite scent or cologne. It's among the most meaningful aspects of exhortation to a significant distance.

6. Be aware of what success means to your

It's hard to know if things are going well in your relationship with a significant distance when there isn't a clear goal that is a top priority. Would you prefer to endure some time of disconnection? You will eventually get married? Continue to be married even though your work assignments are leading you to different areas? Thinking about what success means to you and whether you're getting closer to that goal is crucial when trying to determine whether your efforts are effective or not.

7. Smiling with your friends

in a way which doesn't cause a raise. It could sound risky but a harmless tease like giving your barista a smile or giving a compliment to a stranger could be beneficial to your relationship, as long that you're respectful to your companion, yourself and even the third person.

It's not necessary to shut off your other-worldly side because you're adrift due to separation. In reality, the most happy couples make use of the extra-social aspect of their relationship to fuel their own tease, enticement and sexual flash within the relationships.

8. Do things that your partner does not like doing.

Perhaps you are a fan of shopping, going to the recreation center, or watching movies, but your companion doesn't enjoy anything else. Why not make the most of your time and perform the exact same number of exercises that you'll need?

This is an excellent method to discover a silver cover during your time separated from one another.

9. Let people know about the relationship.

If you're contemplating ways to make substantial connection over distance, you'll have to admit you're connected. The majority of significant distance connections don't seem as authentic like in-person connections.

There's a portion of it because there's still some stigma associated with the issue. To make it seem more normal make sure that everyone who is significant to you in your local area (companions and family members as well as people who have to get to know you) recognizes that you're in a long-distance relationship.

Truthfully, there's no need to speak to your S.O. frequently, but avoiding talking about them or referring to them as untimely is a quick way to diminish your relationship's chance of being successful.

10. You must ensure that you aren't being fished by cats.

This is mainly a concern for people who begin their relationship from a distant location however, with online dating becoming more popular than at any other time in recent history it is crucial to clarify. There are some incredible distance connections, and in all likelihood there are many people that claim to belong someone other than themselves.

Prior to entering into or staying in a relationship that is significant distance make sure that the person you are with is who they say they were.

11. Make sure you're with "The The One."

The principal reason you be in a lengthy distance relationship is the assumption that they are the only one.

It's actual. If you're looking to date for entertainment, it's best to take it up in a local setting.

12. Look for fighting as a positive indicator

This piece of important distance-based relationship advice can be beneficial in the course of a relationship. Everyone has both good and bad moments however, a study revealed that couples that use effective methods of settling disputes by listening to the other's viewpoint and trying to get their partners to laugh were less likely to be averse to separating on disagreements.

As opposed to staying out of the possibility of a discussion that allows you to let a few issues out in the open, take advantage of it to resolve issues in a group.

13. Do not give them the play-by-play.

Why? Indeed, it's exhausting. It's not necessary to divulge every detail of your day so that you don't get lost," O'Reilly clarifies. If you're only going to discuss your plans (what you've accomplished today and what you'll be doing in the coming days) You could be perfectly content to keep the conversation both inside and out.

Refreshes can be important and essential, however when your conversations are reduced to setting goals It's not likely that you'll feel energetic, whether or not you're from each other.

Instead of sharing day by day updates, discuss your most intense feelings of fear or excitement about festivals, and your dreams. Talk about all the things you have to accomplish when you meet."

14. Keep in mind that your partner may not be the perfect person.

Some partners will generally praise their relationship, and will remember that it was better than it actually is. Research has proven that couples who have more respect for their relationship are likely to break up due to an unstable relationship.

If you only remember the positive aspects of the relationship with your S.O., you may be irritated when you have an opportunity to meet another time. Instead of building them up in your head to be an ideal partner, try to stay in the present.

15. Don't be fooled by clever unexpected surprises

It is a common practice to have surprises in any relationship, however the ones with significant distances can benefit more due to they do not have a regular physical contact. Surprises could be anything from surprise visits to small gifts with the sole purpose of causing a hell. Significant distance relationships endure when either of the participants feel that they are neglected or ignored.

Extraordinary treats are more than a text message or call because of the special focus and effort you invested in arranging it.

16. Take into consideration an open relationship

Although they're not suitable for everyone, but when you're really struggling with separation issues an open relationship could help you overcome the loneliness that comes with LDRs.

Dejection is a difficult thing to overcome. If you and your partner are both happy with and agree to the idea, you can both explore other relationships within your vicinity in the process of becoming two. You'll be surprised by the amount of people are interested in meet a committed and loyal person.

17. Don't get hung up on your schedule

There's nothing more painful than listening to someone make a call to their accomplice when it's at 7:00 p.m. Furthermore the conversation is always at 7:07 p.m.

It's so repetitive and confined. If you have to go through this, you need to keep it exciting.

18. Be aware that a negative experience isn't a sign that you're breaking up

If you're in a long-drawn out LDR It's normal to have amazing and unpleasant interactions with your partner. In these and other instances, the pressure of having a relationship for a long time can create tension, however especially when you're keen to meet your S.O. In the event that you're having a meeting that isn't as you expected, don't make an uninformed conclusion about what this means to your relationship.

19. Sexts sent out that require decoding

Sexting is a vital part to being part of a long distance relationship. But, as you can imagine that you rely on proven strategies all things except guarantees will be exhausting soon.

Instead of removing the most smoky body parts, you can send close-ups that require you to alter edges and shift viewpoints in order to see the entire picture. Being a good sport and not letting your partner get into a debate is essential to generating an energetic relationship.

20. Do you have a personal idea?

If there was a local break-up and now in a long distance relationship that you are in, you'll end up with a lot more free time. This is especially true when you had been in a relationship near and now are looking for only one person in a faraway location.

It doesn't matter if it's preparation for a long-distance race or mixing your own beers as well as joining an online bowling team It's an excellent way to do something you're will put your newly gained time.

21. Be aware that LDRs are in reality pretty normal

The research has revealed that 75 percent couples who have drawn in were in a long distance relationship at some point.

When put within the context of the context of an LDR seems like a bit less important.

22. Use a sex plan

It's not a normal thing to discussit, but it is essential to have a conversation. The feeling of being disappointed by sexual partners is among the primary reasons people cheat in relationships that are very distant.

The best way to overcome this issue is to make an arrangement of sexual intimacy. For some couples, it's typical to have video and telephone sexual sex. For others it's an open-minded relationship or similar. There's no ideal one, however, you need one.

23. Let your relationship go for a while. every once in an in

There is a good chance that you have plenty going on outside of relationships, and you should focus around that . Take days during which you stay away from anything that can help you to recollect these moments.

Doing this for two or three days per week will allow you to relax some of the deep bond to the extent that you will miss them less but you will cherish them more.

24. Keep calls brief and sweet

You must be certain that any phone choices, written messages, Skype or Facetime are locked in. Skypeing with your partner while distracted by other activities will have greater negative impact than doing it when you are sitting next to each other.

Be sure to lock it in.

25. Don't use jealousy to gain advantage

In the event that you require an excellent relationship with your partner no matter if it's been a while time ago, you separated from him It's not a good idea to make use of envy to make him want or desire more of you.

It's safe to tell him you're creating good memories even when he's not with you, but don't concentrate on the things that he's wearing that makes him want to be with you.

This won't make your important distant lover want him, he'll find it difficult to trust the relationship he has with you and this could be the beginning of the end of your relationship. It could be significant distance or another.

I'm sure this relationship advice has been stimulating? Examine them, and you'll definitely promote you as having one of the strongest relationships that your colleagues will try to emulate.

26. Accept that change is inevitable

Research also shows that the primary reason of significant distance relationships not being successful is that couples rarely expect sudden changes in their relationship. The length of time you've been separated and the areas you share and the terms of your separation could change over time. Prepare yourself for this and be ready to talk about it instead of to shutting down when faced with an unexpected obstacle.

28. Try having a date that is digital.

It doesn't matter if your loved family member is located 6,000 miles away it is possible to meet up. Instead of calling or having a video chat, you can have an idea of having an enjoyable evening out with friends. Enjoy some wine and enjoy a meal together.

Whatever the case, whether virtual or not or not, it could be a memorable experience. I advise my clients with large distance connections to make plans for this in order to create trust and feel connected.

29. Don't worry about the miles

If you and your companion are within hours of each other, it's not that difficult to observe one another regularly. However we've got a hint of something more favorable for couples who have bi-beach relationships or have global connections.

An analysis published in the Journal discovered that couples who had the additional physical distance between them are likely to achieve better results. Although it could get heated however, it's worth keeping the couple together

30. Set a time limit for the relationship

A lot of people don't like being in an LDR up to the very end. In case you're one of those individuals--amazing. If not, take a look at how long you're willing take to cover the huge distance.

If you agree with your partner in the event that your relationship is not worth staying in, you'll be able to end the separation with either one of you shifting to a more pleasant location. In addition, if your relationship does not develop within the specified time do not hesitate to break off the connection to stay out of anything that's not reasonable.

Chapter 22: The Do's And Don'ts

How many years has your partner and you been in a relationship? If it's been a matter of months or days separation can be difficult.

But having an ongoing relationship that is long distance isn't without its benefits and drawbacks. Nothing will replace the joy of being with someone you love and knowing that they'll be there for you. And just being in a an extended relationship does not mean that your partner won't be there.

It is essential that you keep in touch and inform your partner that you're missing them and remind you that there will come some point when you'll not be separated by distances.

There are a few dos and don'ts to be aware of prior to when your relationship develops into one that is long-distance and throughout your relationship.

Know when the Distance will be Over

The most crucial element of the relationship. It is crucial that you and your partner have a realistic timeframe to consider the point at which you will not be in a relationship.

While it isn't as easy as it may seem , and there will be times when you feel like the day of your departure is a long time away Knowing when you'll be together will lessen the burden of separation.

Discuss it

It is vital to you and your partner discuss the move as well as the expectations and motive behind the distance.

It is common for relationships to come to an end without reason because one of the people in the relationship must leave for work or school and the other believes that the relationship is over.

Discuss it and do not speculate or ask what might happen. Discuss with your spouse if you would like that the relationship will continue to develop when they're away, and share your opinion about the issue.

Let your thoughts be known before both of you live separated by a distance.

Create a Plan

Set a timetable before distances are between you. It is crucial to plan to communicate every day at least once and make use of the webcam as often as you can.

If your day is busy for you both set a time to make a call before the time you go to bed even if it's just a brief "goodnight".

Plan Visits

It is nearly impossible to plan every visit prior to the separation, however it is crucial to plan a date at the beginning of each month to determine to when and if you will be able to visit.

If your budget permits you to do so, it is recommended to meet at least once a month and have alternate visits.

Do not be jealous.

The long distance relationship is notorious for the tendency for jealousy to be a problem So, you need to believe in your partner and the other person has to be able to trust you.

Don't give one another any reason to believe that you are not trusting each other.

Always be honest, speak the truth no matter how difficult it might be. If you're in love and you are certain that you'll be together at some point the issue of jealousy should not be an issue.

Be aware it is a given that you as a spouse are going out with friendsand having fun together, and that's fine. Trust and communication will prevail over any jealousy that you might have.

Make Each Other Surprise

It is a good idea to surprise your partner often. If it's a simple gift from your family, or even a loving note or even you, it will strengthen two of you.

Send gifts to your loved ones when there's no need for an occasion to celebrate or phone your spouse to say how much you love them.

Face to Face

Calls to the phone are great and you should make calls to your spouse every day However, face to face time is equally important.

Join Skype and Video Chat, or whatever you feel comfortable with, as long as you are taking advantage of technology and communicate with your friends frequently.

Negativity

Don't listen to negative opinions of your relatives and friends. Be sure that your bond can withstand the distance.

Chapter 23: Utilize Technology To Create An "Shared" Experience

Write One Boring Letter

Writing letters in hand is a lost art form. It's not necessary to purchase a mahogany table and begin writing correspondences with dukes and duchesses by using feather quills with ink. Simply write a single letter. In reality, it's better to be a bit in the middle. Don't make any grandiose statements regarding how you will proceed in the letter. Keep it in a casual and casual tone, as it were a conversation with one another one-on-one. Share your opinions about different kinds of sandwiches, perhaps or go to an event and then describe the atmosphere. Make it easy. Send the initial draft. There is no need to write in your letter about your feelings since the gesture itself conveys the message in a clear and unambiguous manner. Include a photo. It's not just thrilling (and uncommon) to receive an item like this in your mailbox, but you've put the physical object in the home of your partner. One of my passions over the last couple of years has been graphology, also known as handwriting analysis. As an expert in graphology I'm here with that whether you realize whether or not you write your own personality into every word you write, and even your feelings about your readers and the words that you're writing can be identified by graphological clues. I'm confident that even a letter in which you simply tell some random tale will give the reader the chance to feel the atmosphere of you, the writer even though you're not present. They now have the chance to experience a little of your presence by reading the letter at any time.

There are two risks to be aware of when writing your letters. First, remember that relationships are always changing over time. Make sure you don't make any assurances or other important information that might be called later on. The letter should be considered an opportunity to entertain the person who wrote it. We all have the feeling of guilt that comes with it when someone writes you a letter but you did not reply. Therefore, don't be expecting a response. Additionally, don't write a second one unless there is a solid reasons to believe that the object won't become an issue to guilt and obligation to the other parties. A single letter is sufficient.

Buy a hands-free headset

There are a variety of options on the market for headsets with hands-free capabilities. You can purchase one and test it out. Find your comfort level with it. Some work better when playing music or exercising. My personal preference to make phone calls is the one that has the U-Shaped wand, which fits around your neck , and includes an audio device that rests on your clavicle. Even the cheapest models which plug into your phone's 3.5mm port in your mobile, and come with an extension cable with microphone the other end will work fine and are priced at less than $10.00. Place it in your bedroom. If you are in a relationship that is long distance, there are times when the only contact you have for weeks or more will be the telephone. It is important to make it simple for your body to move and ergonomically. It is an acceptable manner to use your phone to cut down on distractions and keep your focus on your conversation, often at night , you'll be forced to pick between the routine of your evening, i.e. cooking dinner and cleaning up your home or packing for tomorrow or even talking on the phone. With your hands free, you can accomplish all of those things.

General Telephone Use

The phone being used to talk when distracted is not optimal. Make a rule of thumb that when you speak via the phone with your long distance friend, you won't be performing other activities, such as watching TV. Music can be helpful in creating a conversational tone but TV and other things can be distracting and hinder your attention to the call that is your primary method of staying connected with your loved one. If there are other things you must complete or want to be doing you can simply say that and close the phone call. In the next call. Make sure your conversation partner is focused on the conversation or in the event that they aren't able to be able to, gently inform them that you'll talk to them in the near future . Then put the call down. Unfocused and unintentional conversations can cause confusion. Incorrect understandings can result in disputes. Arguments are more difficult to resolve when they are thousands of miles, and must be avoided. In addition, no serious conversation are permitted after 10 pm (whether distant and not). This is the point in the day, and the majority of your physical, emotional, and mental resources are depleted from the day and require relaxation. Establish this rule before the time, so that disputes late in the evening over the phone are prevented at all costs. It's incredible how a good sleeping in can do to alter your perception.

Skype, FaceTime, Pictures Texting, and Messages

I'm not very familiar in using Snapchat except for the receiving end , so it was not on the list. However, there's no doubt that we are living in the most exciting time for long distance relationships as there are numerous ways to share photos or videos of your partner around the world. A five minute video call every month could go quite a ways to keep the flame alive and remind you how hot and enthusiastic about who your love is. There are over 200 muscles that are in the face that transmit information between them when you are in front of one another.

My personal view about selfies is they are unusual thing for a variety of reasons. Instead of just posting selfies throughout the day, make use of your imagination. Send pictures which don't feature your face in the picture. It's not about telling your friend how adorable you are, but it's about creating an "shared" impression. You can share funny things that you have seen. Photograph an old lady you have met and then send it along with a note that says "remind me to talk to the story of Edna". Send photos, videos along with text messages that explain the funny or interesting things that you have to deal with in your day-to-day life. Over time, this will create a sense that you are in a shared space and moving through life together, even if you reside within different towns.

One method I use to text is to engage in three or more conversations or conversations simultaneously, but instead of signing them as one long text , I divide them into three or two texts and then make them the order of a row. This allows my friend to respond in a specific way to the portion they find the most engaging. Be aware that when you text someone, they may be distracted and busy. Also, this technique gives you a more intimate feeling since it closely resembles the casual and unstructured ways that people who know one others well communicate in person, and not as much the back and forth emails. It is possible to take or leave this split rapid-fire texting method, but you should definitely install and get familiar to Skype as well as FaceTime and do not let the application be left on your phone unattended.

Look Up Other People

If you suspect that your partner is a cheater There is no way to stop it. Accept the fact that they are cheating. Take it in. If you're in a long-distance relationship or not that is the reality. Being jealous can be naive. It's not a way to live and be a person of jealousy. If your bond is strong and has strengthened over time, it's a unique and uncommon thing that will be able to stand up to scrutiny. If it doesn't, and you suspect someone has been unfaithful, the other person likely was not guilty of anything. Humans are created to be attracted by each with one another. Accept it. Inspire your spouse to look at other people, urge your partner to join the fitness center. Encourage them to go out to explore the world. And inform them that they are not under any obligation from any obligations to anyone else. It's going to be difficult, but you have to make something completely free if are in love with it. The most important thing you do not want is them at home, doing nothing, and fantasizing about seeing them again. This can lead to feelings of jealousy on their behalf. Encourage others to seek the person out when you have people who have a common interest in their community. It is possible to assume this implies that they might meet someone attractive at some point. However you must resist the urge to ask too many questions. If they ask how their meal was, but don't ask whom they were with. If they don't contact or text you back, don't make any major fuss of it. Try to pretend it never happened. Be sure to give them your space. If you have a strong relationship, let you can trust the relationship. Long distance relationships are difficult. A healthy sense of disengagement is essential. Different people view relationships in the same manner as I do. If this chapter is offensive to you, perhaps you should just pick what you can and forget the remainder. Maybe your ideas regarding relationships are narrow and ivory tower. Perhaps you should take it with a pinch of salt. Personally, I think it's crucial for men to look at other people when in relationships. I'm not suggesting that it's necessary to pursue women around town and degrade your spouse. I'm just saying that a woman the course of a relationship can choose other alternatives. You can't stay away from it, if she attempts. All she has to do is create an Tinder profile and upload two photos or go out for a walk and she's got choices. For men, it's more complex. I'm not saying that you're a fragile person and require reminders that women want you, but I think it's important to spend time with women. This will make you feel less reliant and less jealous of your long distance companion If you have a few women of high-quality. Be a part of the friend zone. Being around other women and going out with you and laughing with your jokes can improve your chances of becoming a great boyfriend , in my view. There are times, in my personal experience, if I'm in a long-distance relationship and meet a local lady and go to dinner or a social occasion that I attend with her am awestruck by my time, but when I leave at the end of the evening, it makes me feel even more thankful for the unique relationship I've developed with my girlfriend. Being around women helps me keep my meter sharp and helps boost my confidence. However, it also allows me to see how they can not measure up to her. The grass isn't as green as it seems from the other end. This chapter may be the most difficult chapter to swallow. It's not for everyone, and so let's return to the step-by-step, concrete procedure.

Chapter 24: Always Be There For Your Partner

Whatever distance you are from one another it is important to have a back-up plan for your spouse when things get tough. Distance isn't an excuse for not knowing the current state of the life of your partner. If you are concerned enough, you'll be able to tell if something is not right since you are the first to reach out or ask questions. If you are familiar with your spouse well, you'll be able recognize that there's something wrong by looking at the text and also by the sombre tone of the voice.

There are numerous ways you can be present with your spouse. One way is to simply pay attention. There are instances where people simply require their loved ones' ears to hear their worries. Just listen attentively and then respond accordingly as your spouse explains the numerous issues that arise at work. If you are not sought, do not provide it. If someone asks for advice They will ask that from the beginning such as 'Hey, I would like your opinion on that ..." and that's similar to this. Sometimes, people have to vent their frustrations with someone who can help them let their minds go and let their minds rest.

Another way to help the other person in your life is to offer guidance when you are asked. If you're asked your advice, it may indicate that your partner is in a state of distress and isn't sure how to proceed. You must be mindful to be able to understand what's happening. When you have a complete story, you are able to offer your ideas that could aid in solving the issue. Couples who seek for advice from one another are trustworthy and respectful in their relationships. This is because you get receive advice from those who you trust and trust.

You can also make your loved one smile and forget about the problems by sending gifts, flowers and letters by mail, or sending an email with a brief message or video or writing a poem that puts smiles on their face. This will let your beloved person know that they can remain in their thoughts regardless of how far away.

There are instances that require you to see your spouse in person. If your partner is injured or is sick and you are unable to reach them, it is best to immediately get onto the next plane or bus to make urgent visits. Whatever you're doing or how busy and if you truly are in love with your partner and realize that this is one that is the difference between the utmost importance, then you shouldn't be hesitant in taking the decision to go visit. Also, you should consider a visit when there's a significant occasion like your partner's birthday, anniversary, or the day of your loved person's high school graduation.

Being there for your partner does not just need to be considered in the midst of difficulties but also for special occasions that your spouse is involved in. Couples must be able to share these moments of their lives with one another.

Conclusion

In this guide , we discussed about the importance of communicating in a relationship that is long distance. How do you deal with an absence of intimacy. What can trust do to be the difference between a long-distance relationship. and discussing how you will continue to grow in your partnership.

If you are in a relationship that is long distance, try to talk to your partner to compensate to make up for any gap between you. Be aware that changes are likely to occur in every relationship and the best way to deal with the change in the long-distance relationship is to communicate with her. Talk to your partner so that she would be happy to talk to you , and also listen to the point that your partner would be delighted to talk to you.

Lack of physical intimacy at the initial stages of a relationship that is long distance is a challenging adjustment However, things like daily conversations, taking photos and offering moral support or having a vivid idea about each other could help in the process of adjusting. The ability of you and your partner to communicate will determine the degree of intimacy you share.

Trust is the foundation of any relationship. You must be honest and transparent in your relationship with each other. Allow each other to have some privacy. Trust your partner. Dispel doubts and miscommunications. Be honest even if it hurts, and you and your spouse will be more understanding and respect each other.

Discuss your future plans with your spouse. One of the best ways to demonstrate the seriousness of your relationship in your relationship over a long distance is to discuss your future as frequently as you can. This increases the confidence of the relationship. If you notice you are drifting away with your partner, be transparent and communicate with your partner. There's no reason to be a leader for your partner.

This guide should give you have a satisfying and happy relationship.

www.ingramcontent.com/pod-product-compliance
Lightning Source LLC
Chambersburg PA
CBHW071838080526
44589CB00012B/1040